A TREASURY OF ARCHAEOLOGICAL BELLS

A TREASURY OF

A Chanticleer Press Edition   Designed by Henry Altchek

Nathaniel Spear, Jr.

ARCHAEOLOGICAL BELLS

Hastings House Publishers
New York

Dedicated to my dear wife Kamilla

Library of Congress Catalog Card Number: 78–67123
Spear, Nathaniel Jr.
A Treasury of Archaeological Bells
ISBN: 0–8038–7182–1

Published in 1978 by Hastings House Publishers, Inc., New York.

Published simultaneously in Canada by Saunders of Toronto,
Ltd., Don Mills, Ontario.

Prepared and produced by Chanticleer Press, Inc., New York.

Printed and bound by Dai Nippon, Tokyo, Japan.

Contents

The Prophecy of Zechariah

*On that day shall [every thing],
even to the bells of the horses,
be holy unto the Lord.*

Zechariah, 14:20

Preface Many books have been written about bells because the subject has always been of universal interest. Some of these books have been about church bells; some have been devoted to the science of bell founding, and some have dealt with the general subject of bells throughout the world in prehistoric and historic times.

As far as the author knows, however, no book has been devoted exclusively to archaeological bells. The archaeologist, bell collector, campanologist, student, and traveler—in fact, anyone interested in archaeological bells who visits museums today—will be disappointed to find few or even no archaeological bells in the display cases. This may not be due to a dearth of bells in the region covered by the museum. Archaeological bells, competing for exhibit space with finds such as marble and bronze statues, pottery, glass, and other treasures, many of gold and silver, are frequently relegated to museum storerooms. However, this situation may change, as more museum curators become aware of the increasing number of bell collectors throughout the world and a growing interest in bells in the public sphere. For example, in the United States, this growing interest is manifested by the existence of the American Bell Association, established in 1940; it presently has more than 2,600 members, living mainly in the United States and Canada but with eight other countries also represented. Their individual collections range in size from about 50 to more than 1,000 bells. Archaeological bells are eagerly sought and constitute a part of all major collections.

In this book, the author has endeavored to explain the spiritual and practical uses to which bells were put in many parts of the world in ancient times, to present their historical background, to point out any similarities in form which may exist among bells from widely separated cultures, and to assist the bell collectors in identifying bells in their own or other collections.

The bells described here include those excavated by archaeologists and clandestine diggers as well as those that workmen, landowners, and others found by chance.

The reader will note that information on the provenance of some bells described in this book is lacking. In certain instances, this is due to the fact that such information did not accompany the objects when they were sent to museums as gifts or bequests from private collections. In other cases, bells were originally obtained from clandestine diggers who withheld information either to protect themselves from punishment or to conceal sites which they had discovered and might wish to explore again.

In this book the term "bell" is applied to three distinct types: a stone slab or flat metal plate, often called a gong, which resounds when struck by a stick, mallet, or baton; a cup-shaped, conical, quadrilateral or ellipsoidal, open-mouthed object, which resounds when its exterior is struck by a stick or mallet or its interior by a swinging clapper; a spherical, conical, ovoid, or pear-shaped object, with or without slits or other apertures in its body. This last type is very often called a "crotal," a term derived from the Latin word *crotalum*, meaning a rattle. It produces a sound when one or more clay, stone, or metal pellets, which roll freely within it, strike against its interior. Such a bell may be cast with or without a suspension ring or rings. When cast with a socket at its base or when affixed to a spike, it serves as a "pole-top" bell, often borne aloft as a standard.

Measurements of bells are recorded to both the nearest 0.1 centimeter and 1/16 inch.

All bells illustrated are in the collection of the author except those portrayed through the courtesies of museums, private collections, and organizations.

The author has divided that portion of this book dealing with Asia into three parts: Far East, Middle East, and Near East, allocating countries and cultures according to geographic location.

Acknowledgments

As I release the manuscript of this book for publication, I wish to express my gratitude to the historians and others whose writings have provided me with much valuable information.

I am especially grateful to Charles G. Sibley and Alfred W. Crompton, Directors, and David Challinor, Deputy Director, The Peabody Museum of Natural History, Yale University, New Haven, Connecticut. They gave me constant encouragement in my work and furnished me with letters of introduction to museum directors in the United States and other countries throughout the world.

My deep appreciation is expressed to the following individuals in New York for their good counsel: Dietrich von Bothmer, Chairman, Department of Greek and Roman Art, Vaughn E. Crawford, Curator in Charge, and Prudence Oliver Harper, Curator, Ancient Near East Department, and Julie Jones, Curator, Department of Primitive Art, The Metropolitan Museum of Art; Junius Bird, Curator Emeritus of Anthropology, and Gordon F. Ekholm, Curator, Mexican Anthropology, The American Museum of Natural History; U. Vincent Wilcox, Curator, North American Ethnology and Archaeology, Museum of the American Indian; and, in London, Terence C. Mitchell, Assistant Keeper, Department of Western Asiatic Antiquities, The British Museum.

For the warm and gracious receptions extended to me upon my visits to their museums, I wish to thank: A. Poljakov, Assistant Director, G. Smirnova, Marie Yedovina, Loudmila Galanina, A. Waimann, and Xenia Kasparova, The State Hermitage Museum, Leningrad; N. Maisova, Vera Rauschenbach, Irina Gustschina, and Elizabeth Doletskaya, The State Historical Museum, Moscow; Franz Fülep, Director, Ilona L. Kovrig, Eva B. Bonis, Éva Garam, and Tibor Kemenczei, The Hungarian National Museum, Budapest; Jean-Pierre Mohen, Conservateur, Musée des Antiquités Nationales, Saint-Germain-en-Laye; Alfonso de Franciscis, Soprintendente, Soprintendenza alle Antichità della Province di Napoli e Caserta, Naples; Mario Moretti, Soprintendente, and Mirella Macola, Soprintendenza Alle Antichità dell'Etruria Meridionale, Rome; Franz Glück, Director, and Alfred Neumann, Museen der Stadt Wien; Bo Gyllensvärd, Director, and Brita Kjellberg, Östasiatiska Museet, Stockholm; Luis Vazquez de Parga, Vice Director, Maria Luz Navarro and Manoli Asensi, Museo Arqueológico Nacional, Madrid; Luisa Vilaseca de Palleja, Museo Arqueológico, Barcelona; Margarita

10 Armendariz de Laris, Museo Nacional de Antropologia, Mexico, D.F.

I wish also to thank the following, who assisted me in acquiring photographs with reproduction privileges: Miguel Mujica Gallo, Founder, Museo Oro del Peru, Lima; Brigitte Menzel and Dieter Eisleb, Museum für Völkerkunde, West Berlin; Jack V. Sewell, Curator of Oriental Art, The Art Institute, Chicago; Luis Barriga del Diestro, Director, Luis Gomez Vargas, and Clemencia Plazas de Nieto, El Museo del Oro, Bogota; Ann Britt Tilia, Istituto Italiano per il Medio ed Estremo Oriente, Rome; Yigael Yadin and A. Rosen, The Hebrew University of Jerusalem, Institute of Archaeology; Takeshi Ogiwaru, Tokyo National Museum; Byung San Han, National Museum of Korea, Seoul; Maria Savatianou, National Archaeological Museum, Athens; B. K. Thapar, Director General, Archaeological Survey of India; Thurston Shaw, Research Professor of Archeology, University of Ibadan; Camille Charles Viguier, Musée d'Art et d'Histoire, Narbonne; Betty T. Toulouse, Curator of Anthropology Collections, Museum of New Mexico, Santa Fe; Frances Follin Jones, Curator of Collections, The Art Museum, Princeton University, Princeton, New Jersey; Katherine B. Edsall, Peabody Museum of Natural History, Harvard University, Cambridge, Massachusetts; Sylvia Williams and Arno Jacobson, The Brooklyn Museum, New York; Alix Wilkinson and Edward Telesford, The British Museum, London; P. Dribbon, British-China Friendship Association; Thomas Quirk, Royal Ontario Museum, Toronto; Andrew Poggenpohl, *National Geographic* magazine; Ki Byung Yoon, John M. Cates, Jr., John Wise, and Billy Omabegho.

For assisting me in my research, I am most grateful to Misako H. Uryu; Kuang-fu Chu, The New York Public Library; Julia Meech-Pekarik, Morihiro Ogawa, Marica Vilcek, Holly Pittman, and Marise Johnson, The Metropolitan Museum of Art, New York.

Plate 1 (p. 12). Bronze bell. England. Roman Period, circa 1st century A.D. *Height 15.9 cm. (6¼ in.), width 9.2 cm. (3⅝ in.), depth 6.6 cm. (2⅝ in.). Patina dark green.*

The Birth of the Bell

The use of the bell to drive away and protect against evil forces and to increase the power of benevolent forces has come down to us through the ages from practically every culture of the world. Man has never ceased to attribute a magical and protective power to bells, a belief—call it religious or superstitious, if you will—which still seems to hold him in its grasp.

People often ask: "When was the first bell created?" The author ventures his opinion that when lightning flashed and peals of thunder crashed in the heavens, striking terror into the heart of early man, he became aware for the first time of an overwhelming power which was manifesting itself in sound and fire. At that very moment, determined to fight back with some frightening sound of his own, he may well have seized his club and smote a rock. In that gesture was created the first bell.

The Migration of Bells

Since time immemorial, bells have been among the prized personal possessions of people traveling by land and by sea. Nomadic tribes, marching armies, itinerant merchants and craftsmen, friars, pilgrims, explorers, mariners, and others have all played a part in bringing about the migration of bells over the face of the earth. Phoenician, Greek, and Roman ships, the galleons of the Spaniards, and other ancient vessels had bells among the goods they carried to far places.

Caravans of camels and burdened donkeys with bells at their necks plodded back and forth over the lands of the East for centuries. Among the paths they traveled were the "silk routes" between Changan (Sian) in China and Antioch in Syria. Stretching westward from Cathay, the principal route split just before reaching Hami, one branch passing to the right, on through Hami, Turfan, Karashahr, Kucha, and Talass to Samarkand, and the other passing to the left, through Tunhwang with its famed Temple Caves, thence via Khotan, Kashgar, and Bactria to arrive also at Samarkand. From there the way led on through Bokhara, Merv, Hamadan, and Baghdad to its terminus at Antioch. Another much-used branch ran southeast from Samarkand, connecting Bactria and Peshawar with Taxila. As time went on, throughout all Asia the horse became man's most important means of land travel; consequently, more than any other domesticated animal it accounted for the widespread migration of bells.

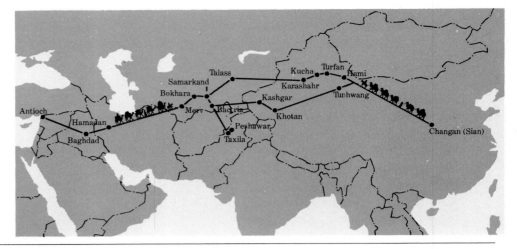

The evidence indicates that the Aryans of the Near East, notably the Lurs and their supposed forebears, the Kassites, began to use horses both in peaceful pursuits and in battle as early as the 13th century B.C.

From the first millennium B.C. nomadism throughout Asia increased steadily until it reached its highest state of development in the first millennium A.D.; and that period saw the vast migrations eastward of the Cimmerians, Scythians, Avars, Sarmatians, Sakes, Huns, and others, as well as the widespread movement of many tribes from Mongolia and Transbaikalia, all greatly dependent upon their horses. The tumuli of most of these people have yielded bells, of both the crotal and swinging-clapper varieties.

An interesting feature in the migration of bells many centuries later was the wide distribution of Roman bells throughout the vast Roman Empire.

Wherever the legions set up their camps and wherever Roman colonies were established, Roman bells were later unearthed. Supposedly discovered in England is the Roman bronze bell in Plate 1 (p. 12), which dates from about the 1st century A.D. From its domed shoulder, slightly concave sides extend down to its ovoid mouth. An iron clapper, of which only rusty fragments still adhere to the interior wall, originally was supported by a ring cast with the bell. That ring is missing. There is, however, a ring replacing the original one, attached with prongs through a small hole at one side of the bell's crown.

For centuries the trans-Sahara trade routes were as important to the Africans as were the "silk routes" to the Asians. As camel caravans laden with goods crossed the desert, the migration of bells was but a natural consequence. There were many caravan routes in Africa. The northern terminus of three historic ones was Tripoli, the ancient Oea, a Phoenician colony, which became a Roman colony after the fall of Carthage (146 B.C.). One route ran south by east via Socna to the Wadai region of Chad, thence east to Darfur Province in the Sudan. A second ran due south via the Fezzan region to Bilma and ended at Lake Chad. The third ran in a generally southwestern direction via Ghadames and Ghat to Timbuktu. From there the route continued southeast and ended at Kano in Nigeria.

An interesting question may be raised on the general subject
of the migration of bells. Was the presence of bells of similar type
and design in widely separated parts of the world due to the fact
that they migrated from their places of origin, or were they
produced in places far apart from one another by craftsmen who
had developed their art independently, entirely free from outside
influence?

Especially noteworthy is the strong resemblance of many crotals
cast by certain Indians of Mexico to those of the Ashanti of
Ghana, as well as a similarity between crotals from Indochina
and Mexico. Whether transatlantic or transpacific migrations of
bells, or both, took place in pre-Columbian times, and if so,
whether they traveled west to east or east to west, is something
on which more evidence is still much desired by many archaeologists, bell collectors, and students.

The Far East

Japan While the carbon-14 method of dating pottery has convinced some authorities that the Archaic Jomon Period of Japan occurred as early as about 7000 B.C., others believe that it dates from about 3000 B.C. However, long before it began, Japan had come under the influence of cultures introduced from Siberia, Mongolia, China, and Korea. From the Middle Jomon Period the inhabitants of the islands seem to have been engaged in a primitive type of agriculture, although they were still dependent upon gathering, hunting, and fishing. Actual evidence that cultivation took place has been obtained from sites of the Late Jomon Period. The Yayoi Period (200 B.C.–300 A.D.), which directly followed the Jomon Period, saw the emergence of a people no longer dependent upon gathering, hunting, and fishing, but with an economy based on the cultivation of rice, especially wet rice. It is believed that the culture which developed during the Yayoi Period was widely shared by the inhabitants of the archipelago and that the Japanese language was already in use. The establishment of rice as a staple food was not the only event to greatly affect the lives of the people. From the continent at this time came a knowledge of metallurgy, resulting in the production of not only implements of warfare, such as bronze spears and swords, but also bronze mirrors, bracelets, and ritual and ceremonial objects, including bronze bells.

The earliest of the bronze bells were given the name *dotaku*, a word represented in the Japanese language by two characters, the first of which has been translated as *do*, meaning copper, and the second as *taku*, meaning a bell-like musical instrument. In a number of Japanese historical accounts which will be cited later in this chapter, *dotaku* have been referred to as copper bells although an analysis of their metallic content has indicated them to be bronze, composed of approximately 80–95 percent copper with the remainder tin, lead, and a minute amount of iron. Some possessed traces of nickel. The prevalent belief is that most of the bells fall within the limits of the Middle Yayoi Period and that they were cast in clay molds. However, no molds have ever been found. Originally created to be rung, they later seemed to have lost their utilitarian purpose and to have possessed only religious significance. At first they were cast in small sizes but, as time went on, larger bells were produced as artisans sought to embellish them with elaborate designs which required greater space. *Dotaku* vary greatly in size, the largest measuring from 4 to 5 feet (1.2–1.5 m.) in height and the smallest from 1 to 2 inches (2.5–5 cm.). In general, the shapes of the bells are similar. Their outer surfaces are usually decorated with crossing bands and geometric patterns, ranging from the simple to the intricate. Many carry line-relief drawings of animals and waterfowl, such as deer, wild boar, turtles, snakes, lizards, and cranes. Others display representations of human beings and their dwellings.

The earliest Japanese *dotaku* displayed Korean influence. The shapes of their bodies, their smooth and undecorated surfaces, and their arched suspension rings were almost identical to those cast in Korea during its Metal Period. Two examples of Korean bells of the Early Metal Period, their clappers lost, are depicted in Figures 9 and 10. In the *World Encyclopedia (Sekai Dai Hyakka Jiten)* printed in Japan in 1962 appears an article written about *dotaku* by Yukio Kobayashi. It states that small Korean *dotaku* had iron clappers. Referring specifically to five Japanese *dotaku*, it reports that three of them were found with copper clappers and two with only their suspension half-rings (*kan*). One of the latter was discovered in Uzumori, Hyogo Prefecture. The encyclopedia further states that about two hundred *dotaku* have been found in the Western Prefectures of Shimane, Hiroshima, Kagawa, and Kochi and in the Eastern Prefectures of Fukui, Gifu, and Shizuoka. Of that number only five were regarded as having been used as musical instruments.

Booklet No. 88, entitled *Nihon no Bijutsu (Arts of Japan)*, one of a series prepared by the Japanese Ministry of Culture, makes reference to a certain *dotaku* which is kept in the Nikko Temple. It describes the bell as having a copper clapper and draws attention to the fact that the presence of a clapper is characteristic of *dotaku* produced during the early period of bell casting in Japan. The booklet also mentions that a *dotaku* with a copper clapper was discovered in Tomari, Tottori Prefecture, and another in Kijima, Wakayama Prefecture. A *dotaku* with a stone clapper was found in Wakayama-shi, Wakayama Prefecture. No signs of wear are visible on the handles of large *dotaku*, such as the one depicted in Figure 1, to indicate that the bells were ever suspended. They carry no target markings to show that they were intended to be struck from the outside. Their bodies are hardly thick enough to withstand heavy blows.

Almost all *dotaku* have been discovered by chance buried in the ground quite near the surface, frequently by farmers plowing their fields. Sometimes they have been found buried along paths and on hilltops. It is generally accepted that *dotaku* were placed in the ground as offerings to guardian deities by fishermen, hunters, and farmers who hoped thereby to be favored with large catches, ample game, and abundant crops; and that such burials were ritual acts performed on various occasions of which the harvest festivals were the most important.

Characteristic of most *dotaku* are the thin, narrow flanges which extend as a continuation of the handle down both sides of the bell. The bell in Figure 1 carries such flanges which decorate its sides with a sawtooth design. Three pairs of small ears protrude from each of the flanges. The bell's handle, similarly decorated, consists of a series of concentric arches, a unique feature of *dotaku*. The author believes that the presence of flanges on *dotaku* are indirectly attributable to Chinese influence, as demonstrated by the presence of flanges on the *ling* of the Shang Period portrayed in Figure 14. The body of the bell in Figure 1 is divided by elevated lines into ten rectangular sections that are of various dimensions and are decorated with ribbon-like designs.

Henry S. Munroe, in a paper presented in 1877 at a meeting of the New York Academy of Sciences, furnished some interesting information regarding *dotaku*. He included in his paper a written statement made by a friend, "a widely read and well informed antiquarian," Yokoyama Yoshikiyo, in which the latter quoted extracts from a number of volumes in a six-part history of Japan, the *Ri'kkoku-shi*, compiled under government auspices and covering approximately the 4th to the 11th century A.D. In at least three places are accounts of the discovery of bells in the ground in different localities at various times. One tells of "a strange and valuable bell" that was dug up in 669 A.D. during Emperor Tenji's reign when the temple of Sô-fuku-ji was being erected in Shiga Prefecture, province of Ômi. Its height was 5 feet 5 inches (1.6 m.). Another describes how in 714 A.D., during the reign of the Emperor Gemmei, a person belonging to the village of Namisaka, in Uta Prefecture, province of Yamato, found, in the

1

Figures 2–5. Gilded bronze bells. Saitama Prefecture, Japan. Late Kofun (Tumulus) Period, 6th–7th century A.D. 2: height 13.3 cm. (5¼ in.), 3: 8.2 cm. (3¼ in.), 4: 3.8 cm. (1½ in.), 5: 3.4 cm. (1⁵⁄₁₆ in.). Courtesy of the Tokyo National Museum.

Figure 6. Bronze ornament with bells. Japan. Late Kofun (Tumulus) Period, 6th–7th century A.D. Overall length of each side 9.5 cm. (3¾ in.), diameter of each bell 3.8 cm. (1½ in.). Patina light green.

uncultivated district of Nagaöka, a "copper bell," which he offered up to the Emperor. It was 3 feet (0.9 m.) in height and measured 1 foot (0.3 m.) across the mouth. Its style differed from the ordinary, and its sound came under the *ritsu* and *riyo* tones. The third account relates that in the second year of Jôkan—corresponding to the year 861 A.D. of the foreign calendar—there was presented to the Emperor, from the province of Mikawa, a "copper bell." It was 3 feet 4 inches (1 m.) in height, and 1 foot 4 inches (0.4 m.) in diameter, and had been discovered in the hill called Muramatsu in the department of Atsumi. It was observed by someone: "This is a precious bell of King A-iku."
The casting of *dotaku* ceased as the Yayoi Period came to a close. The Tumulus (Kofun) Period (circa 300–700 A.D.) followed. Historians now generally divide it into the Early Tumulus Period, which ran from the late 3rd or early 4th century to the last half of the 4th century, and the Late, which ended about the last half of the 7th century. Some historians have seen fit to declare the 5th century as the Middle Tumulus Period. The entire era, especially the 5th century, was characterized by massive tombs, such as those of Emperor Nintoku (313–399 A.D.) and Emperor Richu (400–405 A.D.) on the Sakai Plain near Osaka. During this period communal interest in agriculture lessened and the political power of individuals and clans increased. This led to more warlike pursuits and less devotion to religious matters. Excavations of tombs, particularly those of the Late Tumulus Period, uncovered many weapons and horse trappings, including bells. The era was marked by an increasing use of iron for utilitarian purposes. The four gilded bronze crotals shown in Figures 2–5 belong to that period, and may be dated from the 6th to the 7th century A.D. They were discovered in a *shôgun-zuka* tomb in Saitama Prefecture. The bronze ornament pictured in Figure 6 is also of the Late Tumulus Period. It is composed of three spherical bells joined in a triangular arrangement by short armatures. Single stone pellets roll in two of the bells, but none in the third. In Japanese this object is called *sankorei*, literally "ring bells." It is believed to have been part of a horse's trappings.

6

Korea It is generally thought that the Koreans are a Mongolian race and descended from the Tungusic branch of the Ural-Altaic tribes which over a period of thousands of years settled in the Shantung Peninsula of northern China, southern Manchuria, and the Korean Peninsula. No archaeological remains whatever have been unearthed to shed light upon the life of the inhabitants of Korea during its Paleolithic Age, some four to five millennia ago. However, many finds from Korea's Neolithic Age have been made. These have included ceramics and many artifacts of stone and bone, and tell of a primitive people engaged in hunting, fishing, and farming. Following countless migrations, the country developed a distinct culture of its own. It acquired the name Chosen, and was long to be referred to as the "Hermit Kingdom" because its people stubbornly sought to isolate themselves from outside influences.

At first inhabited by numerous tribes, Korea developed into a group of states which later emerged as the three independent kingdoms of Koguryo, Paekche, and Silla with capitals at Pyongyang, Puyo, and Kyongju, respectively. After long periods of warfare among themselves, the three kingdoms finally came to an end toward the close of the 7th century A.D. and were followed by a series of dynasties.

Foreigners who visited Korea during the latter part of the 19th century were greatly impressed by its natural beauty and spoke of it admiringly as the "Land of the Morning Calm."

Bells made their first appearance in the country during the Early Metal Period in the 5th century B.C. when bronze was introduced from China and Siberia. Korean bronzes also showed strong Scythian influence. Even before the advent of bronze in Korea, the Iron Age had already made its appearance.

The double-headed bronze bell shown in Figures 7 and 8 is of the Early Metal Period and dates to about 400 B.C. It was excavated in southern Korea in the ancient capital of Kyongju. The bell holds two metal pellets, kept in their respective halves of the bell's elongated body by a partition at its midsection. Along the top runs a narrow handle, cast with the bell, and pierced by an irregular oval hole large enough to admit a cord for easy handling. The bell probably is a ritual object used during Buddhist memorial services for departed ancestors.

Figures 7 and 8. Bronze bell. Kyongju, Korea. Circa 400 B.C. Height 5.7 cm. (2¼ in.), length 11.9 cm. (4¹¹⁄₁₆ in.), width 3.7 cm. (1⁷⁄₁₆ in.). Patina dark green. Courtesy of the National Museum of Korea, Seoul.

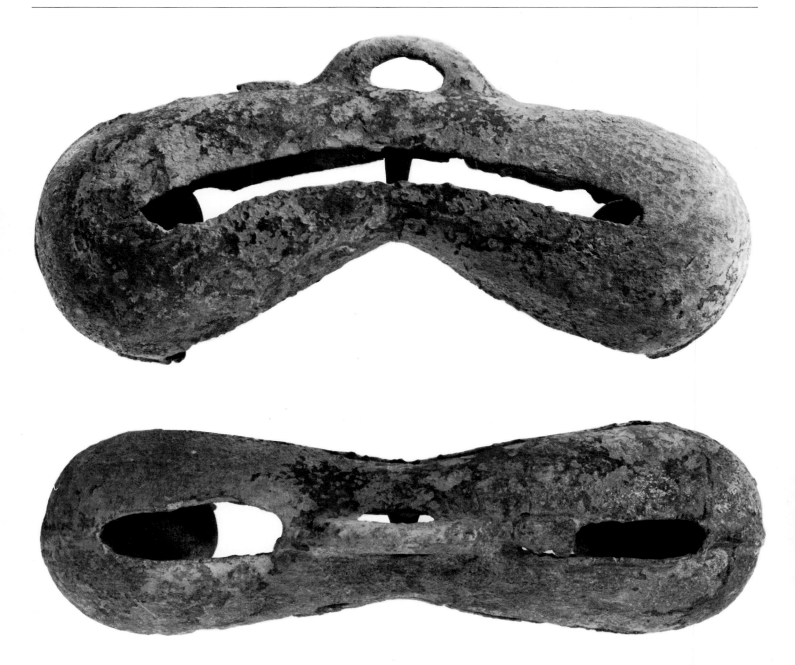

Figures 9 and 10. Bronze bells. Koejŏng-dong, Chunchong Namdo Province, Korea. Circa 500 B.C. 9: height 11.4 cm. (4½ in.), diameter 7.6 cm. (3 in.), depth 5.5 cm. (2⅛ in.). Patina light gray. 10: height 11.1 cm. (4⅜ in.), diameter 7.6 cm. (3 in.), depth 5.5 cm. (2⅛ in.). Patina light gray. Courtesy of the National Museum of Korea, Seoul.

The bronze bells in Figures 9 and 10 also belong to the Early Metal Period and are from the southern Korean village of Koejŏng-dong, Chungchong Namdo Province, near the town of Taejon. Their clappers are missing. They were discovered in 1967 by a land-owner while he was plowing a field. The bells lay in what appeared to be a grave which measured 97‍7/16 inches (2.48 m.) long and 28¾ inches (73 cm.) wide. They probably were used during burial ceremonies and were deposited in the grave as gifts for the deceased.

China

The most ancient bells in China apparently were stone gongs. Such bells are called "musical stones" (*ch'ing*). They have also been referred to as "soundstones" and date back as early as the Neolithic Age, circa 10,000 B.C.
In 1950 a deep tomb of the Shang Dynasty (1523–1028 B.C.) was excavated at the village of Wu Kuan Ts'un, near Anyang, in Honan Province. In it was found the large musical stone shown lying *in situ* on the ledge at the left of the pit (Figure 11).
The outline and features of a stylized tiger couchant are sculptured in low relief upon the *ch'ing*'s polished surface (Figure 12). Though only one such bell was found in this tomb, sets of musical stones, generally much smaller, have been found in many other tombs. For example, during the Chou Period (1027–256 B.C.), they appeared in sets arranged to give forth the notes of a full musical scale. The stones were pitched more closely to the twelve-note octave of the West than to the traditional five notes of the East. The smaller stones were sometimes designated as chimes. The one in Figure 13, belonging to the Warring States Period (475–221 B.C.), was discovered in a tomb at Chin Ts'un, near Loyang, in Honan Province. Its surfaces, which carry no designs, are scratched through use.
Study of the photograph of the tomb in Figure 11 reveals along its eastern and western walls the skeletons in shallow graves of persons apparently put to death in a series of sacrifices during the funeral ceremony—servants and other attendants who were expected to serve the deceased in the hereafter. Not until much later in Chinese history was this cruel practice abandoned. That change in Chinese culture was dramatically demonstrated by a discovery in 1974 at a site in Shensi Province not far from the

Figure 11. Central pit of the Great
Tomb at Wu Kuan Ts'un. Anyang,
Honan Province, China. Shang Period,
1523–1028 B.C. Length 14 m. (46 ft.),
width 12 m. (39 ft.). Courtesy of the
British-China Friendship Association.

Figure 12. Musical stone (ch'ing) from the Great Tomb at Wu Kuan Ts'un. Anyang, Honan Province, China. Shang Period, 1523–1028 B.C. Length 79.7 cm. (31⅜ in.). Courtesy of the British-China Friendship Association.

Figure 13. Stone chime. Chin Ts'un, near Loyang, Honan Province, China. Warring States Period, 475–221 B.C. Length 23.5 cm. (9¼ in.), width 10.2 cm. (4 in.). Courtesy of the Royal Ontario Museum, Toronto.

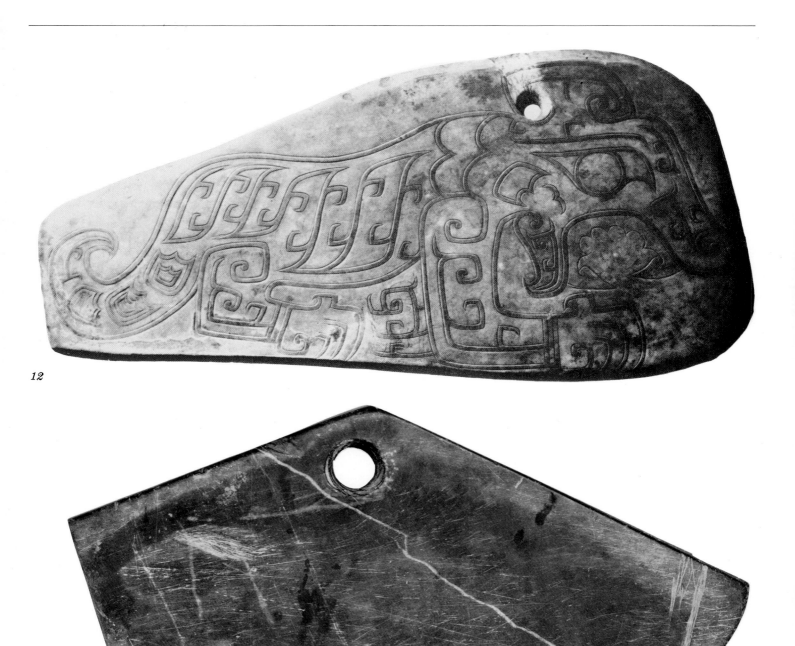

12

13

14

Figure 14. Bronze bell (ling). *China. Shang Period, 1523–1028* B.C. *Height 5.7 cm. (2¼ in.), width 3.8 cm. (1½ in.), depth 3.8 cm. (1½ in.). Patina light green with brown spots, heavy incrustation. Courtesy of the Royal Ontario Museum, Toronto.*

ancient capital city of Sian. At a spot close by the tomb mound of China's first emperor, Ch'in Shih Huang Ti (reigned 221–210 B.C.), Chinese archaeologists unearthed not the remains of executed royal guards, soldiers, or servants, but thousands of terra-cotta, life-size portrait figures of such individuals. Found also were many realistically molded life-size figures of war-horses, together with a few remaining horse trappings and the metal fittings of chariots.

In the center of the great tomb depicted in Figure 11, directly below the central pit holding the inner and outer coffins, a very small pit was excavated. The body of a dog sacrificed at the burial ceremonies was customarily placed in such pits. However, no bones were found in this pit, though the skeletons of dogs have frequently been found in others. It was believed that the dog would guide the soul of the deceased in the afterlife. A *ling* was often found with the dog's bones. A *ling* of the Shang Period, of heavily corroded bronze, is seen in Figure 14. The bell is of oval section with flanges on each side and is surmounted by an arched suspension loop. Identical ideographs stand out in relief on both sides of the bell. The Royal Ontario Museum in Toronto has given an explanation of this ideograph. It is composed of two characters. The one on top is an official rank or possibly the name of a sacred place for the offering of sacrifices. The one at the bottom is a family name. Together they represent a family symbol. Such symbols appear frequently. North of the great tomb in Figure 11, at the top of a flight of four steps, lies a ramp which holds a number of pits containing the skeletons of sacrificed horses. Above the eastern wall, at ground level, stands an archaeologist holding a paper, presumably a diagram of the excavation site. Below, between the musical stone and the central pit, two of his assistants are taking a measurement of one side of the pit, the dimensions of which are 14 × 12 meters (approximately 46 × 39 feet).

It has been widely said that the working of bronze originated in the Middle East as far back as 3800 B.C. and that it was first introduced into China from there. The first bronze bells cast in China appeared during the Shang Period. In workmanship, bells and other bronze objects produced then rank among China's finest metalwork. Customarily, before being put to use, bronze bells were sanctified with the blood of sacrificed animals. Famous bells were often given names. For centuries Chinese custom dictated that bells were to be sounded at religious services and military ceremonies, the type of bell generally used being the *chêng*. The clanging sound of certain bells often led to their use in wartime as an alarm signal and as a way of causing excitement and arousing warlike emotions. Thus, whenever a commander in battle ordered his troops to retreat, he directed that bells be rung, which represented the forces of *yin*, associated in Chinese philosophy with death in nature. Those forces, as the season of the year changed, replaced the *yang* forces, which represented life.

In orchestras in early China, bells had a special function: they were used to give the pitch to the other musical instruments and also were sounded to start the music.

Bells also played an important part in the usually elaborate ceremonies of burial; at the conclusion of the rites the bells were placed in the tombs as gifts for the deceased, together with many other objects, some of immense value, such as weapons, bronze ritual vessels, mirrors, and jewelry. There were also jars (*tsun*) filled with wine, beakers (*chih* or *tuan*), cauldrons (*ting*), and other vessels containing food.

The burial ceremony was always associated with ancestor worship, and it was believed that the sound of the bells and the accompanying music at such ceremonies were heard by and would please the departed ancestors, who, in turn, would send down rich blessings to their living descendants.

Animals were also sacrificed at the burial scene. Figure 15 depicts a chariot burial in a Shang Dynasty tomb of about the 12th or 11th century B.C. The tomb was excavated in 1953 near Ta Ssŭ K'ung Ts'un, a village northeast of Anyang in Honan Province. In addition to the chariot, the tomb contained the skeletons of a charioteer and two horses, together with horse trappings. The horses were of the small kind still used in Mongolia today. The two horses and the charioteer were put to death by special executioners as part of the funerary rites. Within the area where the chariot box rested were found a small bell, a dagger, arrowheads, and two bow-shaped objects. The bell, a swinging-clapper type, is about 5 inches (12.7 cm.) high. Originally, it may have hung directly across the front of the chariot box or just below

Figures 16 and 17. Bronze rein-grip bells. Anyang, Honan Province, China. Shang Period, 1523–1028 B.C. *Length 45.1 cm. (17¾ in.). Patina light green. Courtesy of the British-China Friendship Association.*

16-17

Figure 18. Rendition of author's conception of the use of rein grips attached to charioteer's box of a Shang Dynasty chariot. China.

Figure 19. Detail showing a rein grip in position on the right-hand side of charioteer's box of a Shang Dynasty chariot. China.

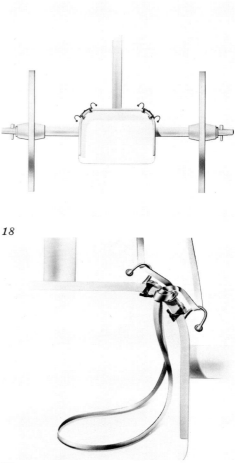

18

19

it. A mystery surrounds the identity of the two bow-shaped objects in Figures 16 and 17. The objects are virtually identical, with only slight differences in the form of the eight-pointed stars which embellish them. Both objects carry a pair of armatures, each terminating in a four-ribbed crotal holding a pellet. Similar objects have also been found in tombs of later periods, and many archaeologists and bell collectors have been puzzled as to what their function may have been. Various theories have been advanced from time to time. One theory was that such an object was used as an ornament attached with bands to a bow. Another theory was that it was mounted on the surface of a warrior's shield. In his book *Archaeology in China*, the distinguished sinologist William Watson describes the excavation of the tomb near Ta Ssŭ K'ung Ts'un as having laid bare the objects in it "in quite undisturbed condition." Mr. Watson's words are particularly significant in the light of the present author's theory regarding the use of the two bow-shaped objects. Figure 15 shows them *in situ*. One is at the right, lying directly across the traces of wood outlined in the soil by the disintegrated chariot box. The other is visible at the rear left inside the box. The curved bases of both objects appear to conform to the shape of the box's front corners, marked in the soil. That they served as rein grips has been questioned on the theory that they could not have been attached firmly enough to the chariot box. The author, after having struggled with the problem for a long time, has come to the conclusion that they did serve as rein grips and the drawings in Figures 18 and 19 illustrate his theory. It is interesting to note that each rein grip was cast with a narrow vertical flange extending about one quarter of an inch below its oval base. That space permitted the base to be fitted snuggly over a wooden block of the same shape attached to or carved in relief on the railing of the chariot box. In order to hold the rein grip firmly to the railing, leather thongs were wrapped around its base. The use of thongs permitted the removal of the rein grips whenever desired. When the chariot was standing still and the two horses, harnessed to the chariot, were standing at ease, tethered or attended by a groom, the charioteer, before descending from the box, would be holding the loops of two pairs of reins, one in each hand. To belay them he had simply to draw each loop across the corresponding rein grip and slip the exten-

Figures 20 and 21. Bronze rein-grip bells. China. Shang Period, 1523–1028 B.C. Length 38.3 cm. (15¹⁄₁₆ in.). Patina light green. Courtesy of the Royal Ontario Museum, Toronto.

sions of the reins under the bell-carrying armatures. The 1½-inch space between each bell and the face of the chariot box allowed the exact amount of clearance needed. Used only while the chariot and horses were at a standstill, the rein grips were subject to little or no tension, and since they were attached near the corners of the chariot box, they did not interfere with the charioteer's movements while he was driving.

Many rein grips terminated in spherical bells. The Shang Dynasty rein grip in Figures 20 and 21, reflecting its association with horses, carries crotal-type bells in the form of horse's heads. Within the partially open mouth of each head rolls a single pellet. The object, including the horse's eyes and ears, is inlaid with small pieces of polished turquoise.

Chariot fittings were usually buried with their vehicles, as in the tomb depicted in Figure 15. But this was not always the case. In *Archaeology in China*, William Watson points out that in the excavation in 1950 of a tomb from the Late Chou Period (473–256 B.C.) at Liu Li Ko, Hui Hsien, Honan Province, carried out under the direction of Hsia Nai, deputy director of China's Institute of Archaeology, nearly all the bronze parts of the nineteen chariots found there, including axle caps, harness-yoke mountings, and shaft ornaments, had been stripped from the chariots before the interment.

Bells of identical form and size frequently embellished the yokes of the two-horse teams used to draw ceremonial chariots in elaborate funeral processions. A bell crowned each of the two yokes. In some instances, a wooden bar was laid across and firmly attached to the yokes. Two additional bells were then affixed to the bar, one to the right of a yoke, another to its left, thus forming a row of six bells in all. Plate 2 (p. 38) shows the front view of one such bell (*luan*) and the back view of another; both are of the Early Chou Period (1027–771 B.C.). Within the elliptical framework of each bell rests a hollow, almost spheroidal section, one side of which has a small hole in its otherwise plain center; the other side also has a small hole in the center from which radiate eight ribbon-like ribs. Within each bell rolls a single bronze pellet. Each bell is supported by a short standard above a rectangular hollow base. There are holes in each base where nails had fastened it to a yoke.

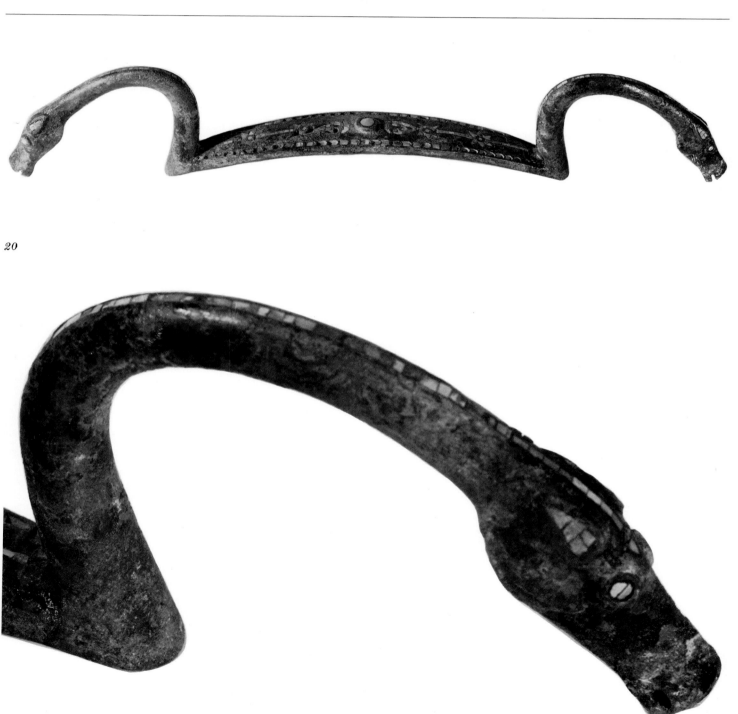

20

21

*Plate 2 (p. 38). Bronze bells (luan).
China. Early Chou Period, 1027–771
B.C. Height 15.5 cm. (6⅛ in.). Patina
light green and azure blue.*

*Figure 22. Bronze bell (chêng) (shown
upended in position for striking).
China. Shang Period, 1523–1028 B.C.
Height 15.4 cm. (6¹⁄₁₆ in.), width 12.1
cm. (4¾ in.), depth 8.9 cm. (3½ in.).
Patina light green. Courtesy of The
Metropolitan Museum of Art, New
York. Gift of Mrs. John Marriott, Mrs.
John Barry Ryan, Gilbert W. Kahn,
Roger Wolfe Kahn, 1949.*

Figure 23. Bronze bell (chung). *China.
Late Chou Dynasty, Warring States
Period, 473–256* B.C. *Height 25 cm.
(9⅞ in.), width 16.7 cm. (6⁹⁄₁₆ in.),
depth 12.5 cm. (4¹⁵⁄₁₆ in.). Patina light
green. Courtesy of The Art Museum,
Princeton University.*

Figure 24. Bronze bell (chung). *China.
Ch'in Dynasty, 221–206* B.C. *Height
60.9 cm. (24 in.), width 25.7 (10⅛ in.),
depth 17.8 cm. (7 in.). Patina brown.
Courtesy of The Metropolitan Museum
of Art, New York, Kennedy Fund, 1913.*

23

24

The *chêng* portrayed in Figure 22 is of the Shang Period. Its handle and body were cast in one piece. No clapper belongs to this type of bell, which was always held in the hand upended—that is, mouth up—and struck on its outer surfaces with a short stick or mallet.

The elliptical *chêng* displayed in Figure 25 is of the Early Chou Period. The entire surface is decorated with owl motifs surrounded by fine, flat tracery replete with spiral designs. At one time these embellishments may have been more sharply defined by inlays of lacquer or some other substance. The handle, which is broken, is not decorated and extends from a flat base with incised designs of two large and two small *t'ao-t'ieh* masks. An almost obliterated design appears on a narrow band just above the lip of the bell.

A bronze bell (*ch'un* or *tui*) of the Middle Chou Period (770–474 B.C.) is depicted in Plate 3. Its loop hanger rests on a flat circular top surrounded by a low vertical flange. Horizontal bands of decorations in low relief encircle both the shoulder and the base. Just above the lower band is an intricate design within a rectangular frame. The bell was sounded by being struck on the outside with a short stick or mallet.

The bronze *chung* in Figure 23 is of the Late Chou Period. Its handle is composed of a flat scrolled bar set upright between a pair of horned dragons, facing each other and sheltering back to back a pair of dragon cubs. The elliptical flat top, and the panels above, behind, and between the triads of nipples, are richly decorated with interlaced scrollings. These appear on both sides of the bell, together with stepped panels of archaic dragon strapwork. In the center of each side of the bell is a pyramidal panel generally reserved for an inscription.

The bronze *chung* in Figure 24 is from the Ch'in Period (221–206 B.C.). It is of pointed ovoid section with identical designs on both sides. It has an eight-sided shank with a suspension loop at the base of the shank on the side opposite that shown in the photograph. In the upper center of each side of the bell is a pyramidal panel without inscription. Each panel is flanked by triads of nipples, with the conventional total of thirty-six nipples. Almost the entire remaining surface of the bell bears a curious Chou design in low relief, except for the lower section, which is

Figure 25. Bronze bell (chêng) (shown upended in position for striking). China. Early Chou Dynasty, 1027–771 B.C. Height 29.2 cm. (11½ in.), width 28.6 cm. (11¼ in.), depth 17.8 cm. (7 in.). Patina green. Courtesy of The Metropolitan Museum of Art, New York, Rogers Fund, 1943.

25

decorated with a faint relief of dragons. Like the bell in Plate 3 (p. 43), it carries no clapper and was struck on the outside with a short stick or mallet.

Such bells were used in creating ceremonial music. They were assembled as a set or chime (*pien chung*) of twelve bells, replacing the traditional set of five, and generally were suspended obliquely in lacquered wooden frames. The first mention of a full set of twelve bells is found in the *Kuo-yü*, a book dealing with Chinese literature and history written about 500 B.C. by Tso-ch'in Ming, who was ranked as one of the disciples of Confucius. The chime of twelve bells was related to the twelve months of the year, each half tone to a designated month. Bronze bells were regarded by the ancient Chinese as instruments of great magical power and were believed capable of attracting the forces of *yin* and *yang*. Of the twelve bells in the musical scale, six were associated with *yin* and six with *yang*.

Various names for the twelve bells are to be found in early Chinese literature. The *Kuo-yü* gives one set of names, whereas an entirely different set appears in the *Yueh-ling*. The following are the names in English of the *yang* bells which have been accepted as proper translations of the Chinese characters used in the *Kuo-yü:* yellow bell, great budding, old and purified, luxuriant, equalizing rule, and tireless. The names accepted for the *yin* bells are as follows: great regulator, compressed bell, mean regulator, forest bell, southern regulator, and resonating bell. The names of these bells became the names of the twelve notes which formed the classical Chinese gamut. The Chinese probably learned to tune bells during the Shang Period, and definitely during Chou times. It is not unusual for an excavated tomb to yield bells in large quantities. To cite but one example, the Chinese archaeological journal *K'ao-ku* tells of a tomb in the village of Pei-hsin-pao, in Pou Lai District, Hopei Province, in which were found parts of a chariot, the bones of dismembered horses, and the skeletons of cattle and sheep together with seventy-eight bells—sixty-five large and thirteen small. In another tomb located in the same village were thirteen small bells. Both tombs date from the 5th century B.C.

Of the Han Period (206 B.C.–220 A.D.) is the bronze bell (*ch'un* or *tui*) in Plate 4 (p. 44). The handle or hanger is in the form of a

Plate 4 (p. 44). Bronze bell (ch'un or tui). China. Han Period, 206 B.C.–220 A.D. Height 49.2 cm. (19⅜ in.) width at shoulder 29.5 cm. (11⅝ in.), depth at shoulder 27.9 cm. (11 in.), width at mouth 20.9 cm. (8¼ in.), depth at mouth 19.1 cm. (7½ in.). Patina mottled light green and dark brown. Courtesy of The Metropolitan Museum of Art, New York, Kennedy Fund, 1913.

Figure 26. Bronze bell (chung). China. Han Period, dated 7 B.C. Height 24 cm. (9⁷⁄₁₆ in.), diameter 11.8 cm. (4⅝ in.), depth 9.7 cm. (3¹³⁄₁₆ in.). Patina brown, some green mottling. Courtesy of The Art Museum, Princeton University.

rampant tiger. The animal stands upon a slightly convex oval platform from which a broad and flaring flange extends horizontally. The circumference of the bell diminishes very gradually as it approaches the oval mouth. Like the Middle Chou bell in Plate 4, this bell was sounded by a blow on the outside.

Also of the Han Period is the bronze *chung* in Figure 26. Within a row of characters inscribed on the uppermost section of the crown appears a date corresponding to the year 7 B.C. The shank is cylindrical and at its base carries a loop for suspension. The conventional thirty-six nipples are present, together with a number of empty panels to complete the bell's otherwise plain decoration.

Inner Mongolia Archaeologists in recent years have talked of establishing a chronology for bronzes, including bronze bells cast by nomads of the Ordos Desert of Inner Mongolia, an area in Suiyuan Province within the northward bend of the Hwang Ho (Yellow River), but nothing has so far been done about this. Some say the Ordos bronzes date from 500 B.C.–500 A.D.; some say around the 3rd to the 4th century A.D.; others declare that the bronzes, especially examples of the "degenerate" animal styles, date well up in the first millennium A.D. A consensus by authorities on the subject would be most welcome.

The author believes that the fact that bells in the shape of stylized pomegranates, the fruit so frequently represented on Luristan bells, appear on certain Ordos horse trappings indicates that they belong to the late 1st century B.C. or shortly thereafter, associating them with the acquisition of Ferghana horses by Emperor Wu of the Han Dynasty. It was well known in China that the finest and most coveted breed of horses came from Ferghana in Luristan, an irrigated region divided between present-day Kirgiz S.S.R. and Uzbek S.S.R. To that breed the Chinese applied the name *t'ien-ma*, "the celestial horse."

W. Percival Yetts, in an article, "Chinese Contact with Luristan Bronzes," in August 1931 in the *Burlington Magazine*, gives an account of a four-year-long effort by Emperor Wu to obtain such horses from the King of Ferghana for use against the invasions of the Hsiung-nu, the Hun nomads of the western Gobi. In 101 B.C. Emperor Wu was finally victorious against the King of

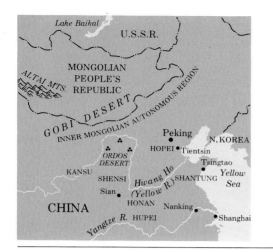

Ferghana and obtained, according to Yetts, "a score or two of superior horses and a breeding stock of lesser quality."

The importation of these larger and speedier horses to China, where only the smaller Mongolian breed had heretofore been used, provided the much-needed military power to establish Han supremacy over China's nomad foes on its northern frontiers. Yetts further states, "The final argument for Chinese contact with Luristan bronzes is, of course, the plausible surmise that the superior horses captured in Ferghana were accompanied with the trappings peculiar to their place of origin." The author is convinced that such was the case, and, furthermore, that after Han cavalry had moved northward against the nomads of the Ordos Desert, Mongolian bell casters saw the pomegranate-shaped crotals on the Ferghana war-horses and copied them. The casting of the ornament with its three crotals of pomegranate shape portrayed in Plate 7 (p. 50) may have been the result of such influence.

In Plate 5 (p. 48) is a short Ordos bronze knife with an openwork hilt crowned with a four-ribbed spherical crotal containing a single pellet. Delicate vertical and horizontal lines crisscross the hilt, which has been cast in one piece with the knife's blade and bell. The knife was purchased in Peking in 1931 or 1932 by Orvar Karlbeck, acting in behalf of the Östasiatiska Museet, of Stockholm. For nearly twenty years Karlbeck had worked as a railroad engineer in China; during that period he developed a consuming interest in Chinese culture and started to collect its archaeological treasures.

The spherical crotals on many Ordos bronzes may have been the product of the imagination of Mongolian bell casters or they may have been copied by them from crotals brought from China anytime after metallurgy was introduced there during the Shang Period (1523–1028 B.C.). Figure 15 depicts a chariot burial in a Shang tomb of the 12th to 11th century B.C. wherein are clearly visible what the author believes to be rein grips. The rein grips are also portrayed in Figures 16 and 17. They carry spherical four-ribbed crotals almost identical to the four-ribbed crotal on the hilt of the knife portrayed in Plate 5. The knife may be dated from the 5th century B.C. to the 5th century A.D.

Plate 5 (p. 48). Bronze knife with bell. Ordos Desert, Inner Mongolia. Circa 5th century B.C.*–5th century* A.D. *Length 16 cm. (6⁵⁄₁₆ in.). Patina greenish black. Courtesy of Östasiatiska Museet, Stockholm.*

Plate 6 (p. 49). Bronze ornament with bell. Ordos Desert, Inner Mongolia. Circa 5th century B.C.*–5th century* A.D. *Height 10.5 cm. (4¹⁄₈ in.). Patina blackish with large spots of calcareous incrustation and, in sheltered places, patches of desert sand. Courtesy of Östasiatiska Museet, Stockholm.*

Figure 27. Bronze pole-top bells. Ordos Desert, Inner Mongolia. Circa 5th century B.C.–5th century A.D. Height 19 cm. (7½ in.). Patina light green with calcareous incrustations. Courtesy of The Art Institute of Chicago.

The graceful bronze object depicted in Plate 6 (p. 49) is conceivably a piece of horse equipment. It appears to have been designed to permit the passage of leather straps at several places. An armature curves upward at one point to support the figure of a stag; it curves in an opposite direction to terminate in the form of a bird's head. Below is a bell in the form of a stylized pomegranate without a calyx. The pellet is missing. At about the same time that he acquired the knife, Karlbeck also purchased this piece in Peking.

The bronze bell in Plate 8 (p. 51) was cast in combination with the figure of a standing ibex. It has particular artistic merit because the animal is very realistic in form, displaying finely executed details. The pellet is missing. Karlbeck acquired this piece in Peking in 1934 or 1935.

The quasi-triangular and flat-sided bronze ornament in Plate 7 holds three crotals of stylized pomegranate shape. It may well have hung below the neck of a nomad's favorite mount. One semi-arched section of the piece has a suspension loop. It appears that the other originally may have had one also, which could have been either lost in the casting or broken off through a mishap. This interesting find was brought to Sweden in 1930 by Frans A. Larsen. Larsen was well known in Kalgan—the gateway to Mongolia. Born in Sweden in 1870, he left home at the age of twenty-three to serve as a missionary among the Mongols; later he became a businessman. For important services rendered to the Republic of Mongolia he was decorated with one of its highest orders and given the title Duke of Mongolia.

Two bronze pole-top double bells of the crotal type, each in the shape of a swan with a cygnet resting upon its back, are shown in Figure 27. There are apertures in their bodies as in the bronze ceremonial bell from Anatolia in Figure 150. Pellets are missing in the cygnets, but single ones roll within the body of each swan. The sockets are rectangular, their dimensions decreasing as they rise from their square bases. The socket at the left is pierced by four rectangular apertures; the one at the right by three. At those points they undoubtedly were attached to poles.

Compared with the number of other Ordos bronzes which have been acquired by museums and private collections, bells are few. As in the case of the Scythians, Sarmatians, Avars, and other

ancient nomadic tribes, the casting of bells by the Mongolians of the Ordos Desert was prompted by a need for horse gear as well as a desire to enhance the appearance of their principal mode of transportation.

India The many archaeological excavations that have been carried out in India during the last twenty years or so have resulted in the discovery of bells of the crotal as well as the swinging-clapper type. Especially active in this work have been the teams from the Archaeological Survey of India, digging at Junapani, Hastinapur, Brahmagiri, and other sites; Deccan College and Postgraduate Research Institute, Poona, excavating at Nevasa, Maheshwar, and Ter; and Nagpur University, digging at Khapa. The bronze bell in Figure 28 was discovered in south central India at Junapani, state of Maharashtra, in a Late Iron Age grave of the Megalithic Culture and is dated between the first quarter of the first millennium B.C. and the 4th century A.D. The bell is of the type usually hung on the necks of cattle. The clapper extends below its mouth, a characteristic of many bells used later during a long period, both in India and in Nepal. Grave goods of the Megalithic Culture customarily consisted of pottery, iron weapons, tools of artisans and farmers, household utensils, and articles of personal adornment in gold, silver, and copper. Shell ornaments and carnelian beads were also frequently found in such graves. The steps taken in preparing a grave such as the one in which the bell was buried and the manner of burial are noteworthy.

After the clearance of the grave site, boulders were placed in a circle around it. The pit for the dead body was dug, the interment made, and the grave goods added. After the soil had been put back, a quantity of soft clay was heaped on it in conical form, reaching the surrounding circle of boulders. Earth and rubble were then added, sometimes completely covering the surrounding circle of stones. Although in many parts of India cists and urns were utilized in burials, and numerous graves were marked by monuments, such as dolmens and cairns, at Junapani only the aforementioned arrangements prevailed. These graves belonged to a people whose language still remains unknown.

Figure 28. Bronze bell. Junapani, state of Maharashtra, India. Megalithic Culture, circa first quarter of the first millennium B.C.–4th century A.D. Height 11 cm. (4⁵⁄₁₆ in.), diameter 7 cm. (2¾ in.). Patina light green. Courtesy of the Archaeological Survey of India, New Delhi.

The Middle East

29

Nishapur Nishapur lies about 410 miles (660 kilometers) almost due east of Teheran. It was an important city during the long period from the 8th century A.D. well into the 13th. Extensive excavations there have brought to light excellent specimens of Islamic pottery. A high percentage of the finds were articles of personal adornment, such as stone and jet beads and delicately engraved stones for seal rings. There were other seals as well, together with vast numbers of coins which presented examples of beautiful calligraphy and design. Though Nishapur was famous as a textile center, excavations in that locality, surprisingly, yielded no textile fragments. Gold finds were rare, and few bells were unearthed.

The bronze bell in Figure 29, reportedly from Nishapur, belongs to the Islamic Period and may be dated from about the 10th to the 11th century A.D. The body of the bell is elliptical and is surmounted by a flat oval platform supporting a rectangular suspension plate, cast as part of the bell. The plate is pierced by a square hole. The bell carries identical ideographs in relief on both sides, and a raised narrow band surrounds its base. Within the bell's crown are two rusted points—the remains of a wire which once supported a clapper, now missing.

Parthia The ancient land of Parthia was part of the mountainous region of Iran southeast of the Caspian Sea and southward as far as the vast salt desert of present central Iran. Eastward, it encompassed an area now called Khurasan. Parthia derived its name from the Parthava, an early tribe of the Scythians. It became a province under the Achaemenian kings (550–330 B.C.) and remained so under the Seleucids (312–164 B.C.). Close to the present town of Damghan lie the ruins of Parthia's ancient capital, known only by its Greek appellation, Hecatompylos, meaning "hundred-gated." The two elephant bells in Figures 30 and 31 were reportedly found nearby, and may be dated from shortly before to shortly after the beginning of the Christian era.

The bell in Figure 31 is identifiable as Indian, particularly by the elaborate design of its rather large suspension ring. This design has prevailed in India with little variation to this day. It has a wide center band, with narrow bands at either side, and small petals which point upward at right and left from the crown. The bell in Figure 30, in contrast, has a suspension ring of simple form.

Figure 29. Bronze bell. Nishapur, Iran. Islamic Period, 10th–11th century A.D. *Height 10.2 cm. (4 in.), width 7.6 cm. (3 in.), depth 6.7 cm. (2⅝ in.). Patina pale green.*

Figures 30 and 31. Bronze bells. Hecatompylos, Parthia, Iran. Circa 1st century B.C.–*1st century* A.D. *30: height 15.6 cm. (6⅛ in.), diameter 11.7 cm. (4⅝ in.). 31: height 15.2 cm. (6 in.), diameter 11.1 cm. (4⅜ in.). Patina light green.*

30-31

Of unusual interest are the pair of very small, identical, female masks that rest close together in relief on the upper part of the bell's waist. The fact that these motifs display hairdos of a form often found on Buddhistic stone carvings suggest that the bell may have originated in an ancient center of Buddhism in India or, perhaps, in the neighboring province of Gandhara, now a part of Afghanistan and Pakistan.

The small-eared elephant, brought to the Near East from India, was used in battle together with the large-eared African elephant, initially in North Africa and subsequently in southern Europe. Elephants generally were placed in the front line of attack. Armored towers mounted atop these huge animals provided excellent vantage points from which sharpshooting bowmen picked off enemy leaders on the field below. The clanging of bells, hung from chains at the necks of the beasts, added to the confusion, as their ponderous frames charged into the ranks of the enemy and trampled the infantry. Their scent, repulsive to the horses, turned back the cavalry and often sent it into full retreat. At the same time in history that elephants were being used in combat, camels were serving a similar purpose. Bells were also hung from their necks. Cyrus the Great (600?–529 B.C.) knew that both the sight and the smell of camels were offensive to horses. In combat with Croesus he placed his camels in the front ranks. As a result, the Persians gained a crushing victory over the Lydians on the plain before Sardis and drove them back to stand siege behind the walls of their mighty capital. Sardis fell in 546 B.C., and Croesus, the last king of the Lydians, was taken captive.

Persepolis Persepolis, capital of ancient Persia, lies thirty miles (forty-eight kilometers) northeast of the present city of Shiraz. The construction of its magnificent palaces was begun by Cyrus the Great; other buildings were added by Darius I (558?–486 B.C.) and Xerxes I (519?–465 B.C.). Persepolis was put to the torch and practically destroyed by Alexander the Great in 331 B.C. Of all the palaces built in Persepolis none was more beautiful or more important than the Great Palace of Audience, the Apadana, built by Darius I. The Apadana was an architectural masterpiece, a gem of Achaemenian art; the very ruins defy description. Two

Figure 32. Bronze horse bell. Persepolis, Iran. Circa 5th century B.C. Height 8.9 cm. (3½ in.), width 5.4 cm. (2⅛ in.), depth 5.4 cm. (2⅛ in.). Patina mottled brown and light green.

imposing stairways on the north and east lead to the Apadana. On their façades are a series of delicately sculptured bas-reliefs, a number of which depict delegations from countries under the suzerainty of the Persian Empire bringing gifts to the monarch. The presence of bells around the necks of the camels and horses brought as tribute, and portrayed on some of those bas-reliefs, is evidence that many bells reached Persepolis from distant lands. In spite of this and the fact that normally many also were among the trappings of horses brought back as spoils of war, very few bells have been found in Persepolis. The absence there of other kinds of bells may be explained by what has been related by the ancient Greek historian Herodotus; namely, that the Persians had neither temples nor altars, their practice being to ascend high mountains and to offer as sacrifices there the boiled or baked flesh of domestic animals. The manner of conducting religious services was in direct contrast to the custom of the ancient Greeks and Romans, who worshipped within temples and who brought to the sanctuaries many bells as votive gifts.

Figure 33 shows a 5th century B.C. bronze horse bell reportedly found at Persepolis. Its four flat and heavily incrusted sides recede abruptly as they rise to a damaged crown below an arched suspension loop. The clapper is missing.

On the uppermost panel of the right wing of the eastern stairway façade of the Apadana appears a bas-relief of a stallion being directed by a Median groom (Figure 34). A comparison of the bell in Figure 33 with the one shown hanging low from the animal's neck on the bas-relief reveals a close similarity in shape and size.

32

Also reportedly found at Persepolis is the bronze horse bell depicted in Figure 32. It is quadrilateral with broad surfaces that recede gradually to a narrow crown. Each of the two broader sides of the bell is perforated by two triangular apertures, their apexes pointing upward, whereas each of the narrower sides carries but one. There are two square holes in the crown where the clapper, now missing, was suspended.

The bronze bell in Figure 36, reportedly from Persepolis, is dome-shaped and has a flat suspension ring with smoothly rounded edges. Below the bell's crown and directly opposite one another are two small holes into which a round bar originally was

Figure 33. Bronze bell. Persepolis, Iran. 5th century B.C. Height 10.2 cm. (4 in.), width 5.7 cm. (2¼ in.), depth 5.1 cm. (2 in.). Patina dark green.

Figure 34. Bas-relief of Median groom conducting a stallion as tribute. Right wing, eastern stairway façade, Apadana Palace. Persepolis, Iran. Courtesy of Giuseppe and Ann Britt Tilia.

Figure 35. Bas-relief, Scythian conducting a horse wearing a bell. Eastern stairway façade, Apadana Palace. Persepolis, Iran. Courtesy of Giuseppe and Ann Britt Tilia.

Figure 36. Bronze bell. Persepolis, Iran. Circa 5th century B.C. Height 7.3 cm. (2⅞ in.), diameter 5.1 cm. (2 in.). Patina light green, partially incrusted with soil.

Figure 37. Bas-relief, Bactrian leading a camel in a tribute procession. Eastern stairway façade, Apadana Palace. Persepolis, Iran. Courtesy of Giuseppe and Ann Britt Tilia.

36

37

Figure 38. Bas-relief, chariot of Darius I. Eastern stairway façade, Apadana Palace. Persepolis, Iran. Courtesy of the Instituto Italiano per il Medio ed Estremo Oriente, Rome.

Figure 39. Bronze bell. Gurgan, Iran. Sassanian Period, 6th–7th century A.D. *Height 9.5 cm. (3¾ in.), diameter 6.3 cm. (2½ in.). Patina light green.*

38

riveted to hold a swinging clapper. Neither bar nor clapper
remains. The bell resembles the one worn by the camel on the
bas-relief depicted in Figure 37 as it advances in a tribute
procession, led on a rope by a Bactrian attendant.
Figure 35 reproduces a bas-relief from the eastern stairway
façade showing a horse wearing a bell and being conducted by a
helmeted Scythian.
Elsewhere on the same façade appears the bas-relief shown in
Figure 38. On it is seen a chariot of Darius I drawn by a pair of
stallions. A bell is visible at the neck of one of them.

Much of Sassanian history is veiled in legend. In fact, it was from
a legendary hero, Sassan, that the dynasty derived its name. The
dynasty supposedly had its beginning early in the 3rd century A.D.
in the province of Fars in southwestern Iran, no great distance
from Persepolis and the palaces of the Achaemenids which
Alexander the Great had left in ruins in 331 B.C.
In the year 224 A.D. King Ardashir I (reigned 224–240 A.D.),
son of Papak, a prince of Fars, administered a crushing defeat to
the forces of the last Parthian king, Artabanus V. After having
established his capital at Ctesiphon, south of Baghdad, Ardashir
lost no time in gaining control over the entire Parthian empire.
The Sassanian empire was further expanded by Ardashir's son,
King Shapur I (reigned 240–272 A.D.). Shapur soon increased the
efficiency of his already powerful fighting forces by modeling his
cavalry after that of the Parthians. Moving eastward, he succeeded in bringing under Sassanian sovereignty Bactria, Gandhara, and the Kushan Empire as far as the important cities of
Kashgar, Soghd, and Tashkent. In the west he extended his empire
to include all the territory of ancient Assyria and Babylon, as
well as Syria and Anatolia. Though subjected to intermittent
setbacks, the Sassanian Empire advanced to reach the heights of
its glory during the 6th century. Finally, however, following a
series of disastrous defeats in battle and the assassination of King
Yezdegerd III near Merv in 651 A.D. the four-hundred-year-old
Sassanian Empire came to an end, and the disorganized states
which survived soon fell before the onslaught of Arab hordes.
The bronze bell in Figure 39 was reportedly found at Gurgan,
Iran. It belongs to the Sassanian Period and may be dated from

The Sassanians

39

the latter part of the 6th to the beginning of the 7th century A.D. Just above the mouth of the bell, which is ovoid, runs a narrow band in low relief. The bell's outer surface is divided into eight panels, four narrow alternating with four wide ones. These extend upward to the crown to meet a flat suspension plate pierced by a round hole. Four vertical motifs, similar but very much narrower than those on the Islamic bell in Figure 151, stand out in sharp relief on the wider panels. The clapper is missing but minute parts of a suspension wire, placed in the mold when the bell was cast, remain.

Susiana The ruins of Susa, the ancient capital of the surrounding area called Susiana (Elam in the Bible), are situated on the Karkheh River about 130 miles (209 kilometers) north of present-day Abadan. Moslem tradition states that the tomb of the prophet Daniel lies in the bed of the Karkheh.

Susa's existence goes back to the Chalcolithic Period, and it was an important center as early as the fourth millennium B.C. Sargon of Akkad subdued Elam in two campaigns about 2320 B.C. The city of Susa continued as the capital until late in its history when it served as the chief residence of Darius I and the succeeding line of Achaemenian kings.

The site was identified as early as 1850 by the English archaeologist W. K. Loftus, but excavations of the citadel were not begun until 1897. The initial excavations were carried out under the direction of the French archaeologist J. de Morgan. There, in the winter of 1901–02, occurred the exciting discovery of the Code of Hammurabi, which had been brought to Susa by Elamites from their victorious campaigns in Babylonia. French archaeologists, led by Jean Perrot, are presently engaged in excavations at Susa. Reportedly discovered at Susa is the conical-shaped bronze horse bell in Figure 41. Its circular flat bottom is perforated by six small apertures. Seven ribs rise to an apex—pierced for a suspension ring, now missing. The bell contains one pellet.

Also reportedly found at Susa are the two bronze chariot bells shown in Figure 40. They are almost identical in size. Each displays a smooth and shiny surface. The bells differ in their openwork designs. The bell at the left has a band, incised with two fine lines, which divides the bell's eight straight ribs equally. The

Figure 40. Bronze chariot bells. Susa, Iran. Circa 1000 B.C. Left: length 12.1 cm. (4¾ in.). Right: length 12.4 cm. (4⅞ in.). Patina mottled dark green and dark brown.

Figure 41. Bronze bell. Susa, Iran. Circa 1000 B.C. Height 7.6 cm. (3 in.), diameter 5.1 cm. (2 in.). Patina light green.

40

41

bell at the right differs from the other in that it has seven ribs cast in a zigzag pattern. Each bell contains two metal pellets. Rings at the ends of each bell permit it to be suspended horizontally across the front of a chariot. Such a sonorous object was hung there to cause fear and confusion in the enemy's ranks as chariot and driver, with one or more archers, rolled into battle.

Similar bells have been unearthed in nearby Luristan. A Luristan chariot bell of somewhat larger size than the two just described is depicted in Plate 14 (pp. 92–93).

Amlash   The culture of ancient Amlash thrived during a comparatively short period from near the end of the second millennium B.C. into the beginning of the first. The site, in the province of Gilan, lies near the southwestern shore of the Caspian Sea in a mountainous area which supports part of the Iranian plateau. There, altitudes rise to approximately 6,000 feet (1,800 meters). On the mountains nearest the sea it rains throughout most of the year. Consequently, due to the prevailing dampness of the soil, many bells excavated in the area show much corrosion. An example of such a bell is shown in Figure 42. It is surmounted by the diminutive figure of a zebu. Its pellet is a pebble. Another bell from Amlash, seen in Figure 43, contains a single pellet and is suspended on a heavy bronze chain, 49½ inches (125.7 cm.) in length, made up of sixty-four links.

In Figures 44 and 45 are two examples of horse bells. Though a corroded condition is characteristic of many Amlash bells, the bell depicted in Figure 45 has a smooth surface entirely free of corrosion and displays a rich dark green patina. Originally, a rod to support the clapper stretched across the shoulder of the bell and was riveted in place. Though both rod and clapper are missing, the holes for the rod are still visible. Opposite one another in the middle of the bell's mantle are two triangular apertures, their apexes pointing upward. There is also a slit which rises about halfway up the mantle from the bell's mouth. The bell's tone was determined by the size and location of the two triangular apertures and by the length of the slit. The bell is suspended by a heavy copper wire twisted into a double loop which passes through the bell's suspension arch.

The bell in Figure 44 has a mottled, dark brown and green

Figure 42. Bronze bell. Amlash, Iran.
Circa 10th century B.C. Height 6 cm.
(2⅜ in.), diameter 2.7 cm. (1¹⁄₁₆ in.).
Patina light green, incrusted with soil.
On loan to The Metropolitan Museum
of Art, New York.

Figure 43. Bronze bell. Amlash, Iran.
Circa 10th century B.C. Height 7.1 cm.
(3 in.), bronze chain 64 links.

patina. The clapper is missing. Originally, it was suspended by
a wire which passed through two small holes in the bell's crown.
The slit in the bell's mantle extends comparatively higher than the
one in the bell in Figure 45. Cast in low relief just above the bell's
mouth run three concentric narrow bands.
The author believes that the odd-shaped, crotal-type bells
shown in Figures 46 and 47 are war-chariot bells from Amlash.
They came into his collection via the markets of Beirut,
Lebanon. Both bells are very heavily corroded. A war chariot
might well have carried such a bell, hung under the box. The
mid-section of the bell has the shape of an axle which is
capable of being rotated when suspended horizontally from
brackets. Below is a cage-like section to hold a pellet or
pellets, now missing. Similar to the bell from Susa depicted in
Figure 41, apertures appear on the circular bottom of each bell.
With the movement of the chariot, the bell could swing freely
to and fro, and ring. Such action would be facilitated by the
difference between the slightly lighter weight of the long
vertical stem extending upward from the center of the "axle" and
the heavier weight of the lower cage-like section containing
the pellet. After each ringing, the bell would gravitate to
its original vertical position. Figure 47 shows one of the
bells lying on its side. Directly beneath its cage-like
section is the form of a recumbent ibex. Its right horn and
body, in spite of heavy incrustation, are still distinguishable.
A bronze bell from Amlash, surmounted by the likeness of a dove,
is shown in Figure 48. It resembles, to a degree, two of the
Luristan bells depicted in Figure 88 in that its eleven ribs are
connected to one another at their midsections by crossbars. On the
other hand, like the Amlash bell portrayed in Figure 42, this one
differs from two of the Luristan bells in Figure 88 in that the pomegranate calyx is absent. The hole just below the dove permits the
bell to be worn as a pendant.
The body of the four-ribbed bronze bell shown in Figure 49 is
also of pomegranate form and is surmounted by the head of a stag.
Its long neck is pierced by a small hole, so that it, too, may be worn
as a pendant.
The bronze bells portrayed in Figures 50 and 51 both date from
the early first millennium B.C. The one in Figure 50 is a conical-

43

Figure 44. Bronze bell. Amlash, Iran. Circa 9th century B.C. Height 8.6 cm. (3³⁄₈ in.), diameter 5.1 cm. (2 in.). Patina mottled dark brown and green.

Figure 45. Bronze bell. Amlash, Iran. Circa 9th century B.C. Height 6.7 cm. (2⁵⁄₈ in.), diameter 5.4 cm. (2¹⁄₈ in.). Patina dark green.

Figure 46. Bronze bell. Amlash, Iran. Circa 9th century B.C. Height 19.7 cm. (7⁷⁄₈ in.), width 8.9 cm. (3¹⁄₂ in.). Patina light green, incrusted with soil.

Figure 47. Bronze bell. Amlash, Iran. Circa 9th century B.C. Height 17.1 cm. (6³⁄₄ in.), width 7.3 cm. (2⁷⁄₈ in.). Patina light green, incrusted with soil.

Figure 48. Bronze bell. Amlash, Iran. Circa 9th century B.C. Height 7.6 cm. (3 in.). Patina light green.

Figure 49. Bronze bell. Amlash, Iran. Circa 10th century B.C. Height 5.4 cm. (2¹⁄₈ in.). Patina light green.

44-45

46-47

Figure 50. Bronze bell. Amlash, Iran.
Early first millennium B.C. *Height 10.3*
cm. (4¹⁄₁₆ in.), diameter 7 cm. (2¾ in.).
Patina light green.

Figure 51. Bronze bell. Amlash, Iran.
Early first millennium B.C. *Height 12.1*
cm. (4¾ in.), width 8.8 cm. (3⁷⁄₁₆ in.),
depth 7 cm. (2¾ in.). Patina light
green. Courtesy of the Trustees of The
British Museum, London.

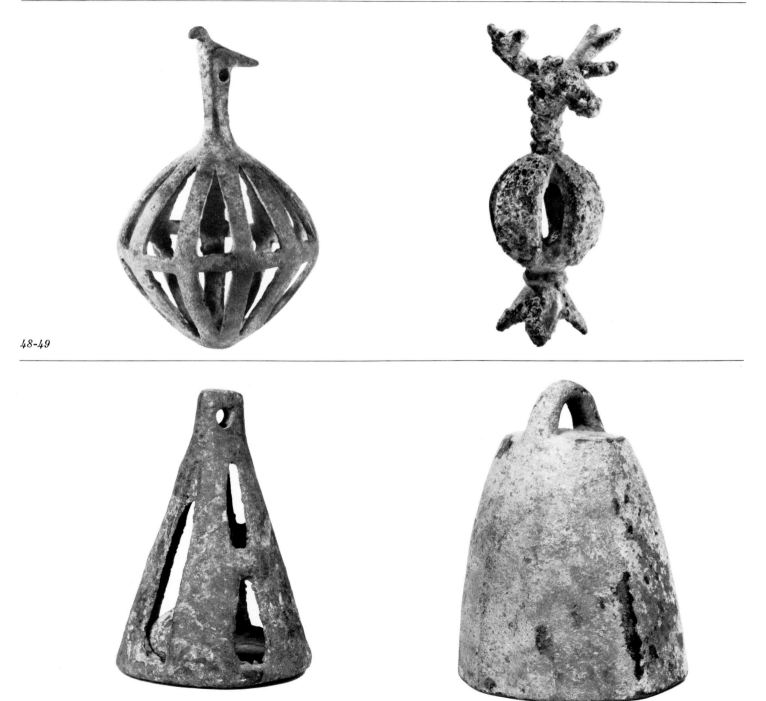

48-49

50-51

Figure 52. Bronze bell. Djönü, Azerbaidzhan S.S.R. Russian Talish, second half of the 13th century B.C. *Height 5.3 cm. (2⅛ in.), diameter 2.2 cm. (¹⁵⁄₁₆ in.). Patina light green. Courtesy of the Musée des Antiquités Nationales, Château de Saint-Germain-en-Laye (Yvelines), France.*

Plate 9 (p. 75). Bronze pendant with bells. Iranian Talish, circa 10th century B.C. *Height 8.6 cm. (3⅜ in.), length 8.1 cm. (3⅛ in.). Patina light green. Bells: height 1.3 cm. (½ in.).*

shaped crotal. Its bottom is pierced by a series of small apertures radiating from the center. The bell's body contains two large and four small vertical openings. There is a round hole at the top for suspension. A single pellet is present. The bell in Figure 51 is of octagonal shape with arched suspension ring. The clapper, which originally hung from two holes in the oval-shaped top, is missing.

Talish   Ancient Talish occupied an area along the coast of the southwestern corner of the Caspian Sea. The northern part, approximately one half of the entire country, lay in what is now the Azerbaidzhan S.S.R. Lenkoran is still the principal town. The southern part fell within present-day northwestern Iran and included the town of Ardebil. Talish lasted from about the early part of the fourth to about the end of the first millennium B.C. The bronze bell with bronze ring attached shown in Figure 52 comes from excavations at the necropolis of Djönü carried out in 1896 under the direction of J. de Morgan.

Djönü is a small hamlet in Russian Talish, less than five miles (eight kilometers) from the Caspian coast. This bell, according to Claude F. A. Schaeffer, dates from about the last half of the 13th century B.C. Its beauty is enhanced by three narrow bands, graduated in size, which encircle the bell between the suspension ring and the crown, and also by groups of deep vertical grooves, which divide its surface into four convex panels. The clapper, now missing, hung from a bar, which still remains in place high within the body of the bell. The wall of the bell is quite thick. When struck lightly from the outside, it emits a pronounced ring.

In Plate 9 (p. 75) is portrayed a bronze pendant from Talish in the stylized form of a standing stag. From its erect head rise six-pointed antlers. Its legs terminate in four-ribbed, crotal-type bells instead of natural cloven hoofs. The conventional pellets are missing. Cast in bold relief and lying horizontally on each side of the animal's body is what appears to be the diminutive form of a crotal. At the center of the animal's back is a loop for suspension. Many bronze pendants in the form of standing stags have been excavated from Early Iron Age graves in the necropolis of Samthavro and other places in the Caucasus such as Djönü, Tülü, and Hivéri in Russian Talish. However, those objects were not cast with bells at the extremity of their hoofless legs. Examples

with bells are rare indeed. It seems reasonable to assume
that the pendant in Plate 9 which carries crotals, may be of
Iranian Talish rather than of Russian Talish provenance. Crotals
were then prevalent throughout nearby Luristan, whence that
type of bell could readily be introduced into Iranian-Talish
territory.

Luristan In 1927, an Iranian peasant roaming in the Zagros Mountains, in
the northwestern part of the range known as Luristan, discovered
by chance the ancient grave of one of his forebears. Within its dust
lay artifacts of the distant past. Almost immediately, clandestine
digging for "treasure" was begun by the excited local inhabitants.
The resultant finds showed that the early Lurs had taken pains to
place within their graves many of those objects which not only
men and women but also children had used in everyday life—
evidence of their firm belief that life continued after death.
Except for the objects which the graves yielded, no record was
found of the history of those people or of their culture—no written
word, no stone sculpture, no paintings or drawings to reveal
something of their religion or their mores, and no dwellings. To
determine their origin and the exact dates of the history of the
Lurs is extremely difficult. It is generally believed that they are
descended from the ancient Kassites. In the opinion of many
archaeologists, their history was confined to the 9th and 8th
centuries B.C., but some declare that Lur culture extended well
into the 7th century B.C.
The Lurs are believed to have been a hardy, semi-nomadic people,
herdsmen who spent much of their time in the breeding and
training of horses. To them horses were essential and, consequently, highly prized possessions. The Lurs engaged in tribal
warfare and predatory raids as they moved about. It is thought
that they lived in goatskin tents and seasonally shifted their abodes
back and forth from the plateaus to the broad valleys of the Zagros
range.
Lur graves have yielded many votive objects, articles of personal
adornment, weapons, much equine equipment and trappings,
including many bronze bells of high copper content. Among the
articles of adornment frequently found in the graves of women
were long bronze pins, such as the one seen in Figure 53. It is

Figure 53. Bronze pin. Luristan, Iran. 9th century B.C. Length 22.6 cm. (8⅞ in.), width 1.9 cm. (¾ in.). Patina light green. Courtesy of The University Museum, Philadelphia.

Figure 54. Bronze pin. Luristan, Iran. Circa 9th century B.C. Height 10.1 cm. (4 in.). Patina dark green.

Plates 10 and 11 (pp. 78–79). Bronze bell pendant. Luristan, Iran. 9th–8th century B.C. Height 7 cm. (2¾ in.). Patina light green.

crowned by a crotal-type bell of ellipsoidal form, decorated with vertically and horizontally incised lines. There is a small knob at the top of the bell and multiple narrow bands at the bottom. In Figure 54 is shown the upper part of a bronze pin. It is topped by a crotal surmounted by the head of a bull. Two pellets are present. It appears that the lower part of the pin was broken off and lost. Because of the thickness of its shank, the pin may have been used on a heavy wool garment. A beautiful bronze bell with a smooth, light-green patina is shown in Plates 10 and 11 (pp. 78–79). This piece of women's jewelry, fashioned to be worn as a pendant, is surmounted by the head of a doe, behind which rests a vertical suspension loop cast as part of the bell. The body of the bell is in the flattened form of a stylized pomegranate with stylized calyx. A series of eight ribs radiates from a central point to form its reverse side, while on both sides of the object appear stylized representations of numerous pomegranate seeds. No pellet is present.

In Figures 55 and 56 are two delicate objects, different in size and arrangement, but otherwise similar. They are possibly women's earrings that were worn in the usual manner or, perhaps because of their weight, were suspended from the head to hang below the ear. The object in Figure 56 has a cup-shaped bell at its top which shows traces of silver laid over a copper base. This indicates that its entire surface had once been covered with silver. Incised on this bell appear three separate groups of concentric circles. It is also possible that both of these objects were hung over a cradle for the amusement and protection of a baby. The almost universal belief in the power of bells to ward off evil spirits has existed since time immemorial. It has prompted not only the making of single bells but also the placing of groups of them on babies' rattles. In Europe, arrangements of small bells have been hung over babies' cradles. In Great Britain, they are called "fascinators." In both silver and gold they were also prevalent in Spain during the 17th and 18th centuries.

Figure 57 shows a bell surmounted by identical back-to-back effigy masks of the mythical hero Ea-Bani; and Figure 58 shows the horned head of the hero fighter Gilgamesh. Both of these objects were cast so that they could be worn as amulets or held in the hand as children's rattles.

54

55   56

*Figures 55 and 56. Bronze ear orna-
ments with bells. Luristan, Iran. Circa
9th century B.C. 55: length 11.1 cm.
(4⅜ in.). Patina light green. 56: length
15.5 cm. (6⅛ in.). Patina dark green.*

*Figures 57 and 58. Bronze bells. Luri-
stan, Iran. Circa 9th century B.C. 57:
height 4.5 cm. (1¾ in.). Patina light
green. 58: height 5.1 cm. (2 in.). Patina
dark green.*

58

57

Many bells in Luristan have been unearthed from rider-horse
graves. When a warrior and his horse died together, the Lurs
frequently buried them in the same grave, along with the horse's
equipment and the warrior's weapons. To honor him as a horse-
man, the warrior's head was placed to rest upon a horse's bit. Even
when he was buried alone, a cavalryman's status was so
symbolized, whether other equine equipment was included or not.
Horse burials also prevailed among the Mongols, Chinese, Avars,
Scythians, Greeks, and others—but never among the Romans.
Within the ten years following the discovery of the first Lur
grave, scores of cemeteries were plundered, and the bells
unearthed found a ready market in the bazaars of Kermanshah,
Hamadan, and other nearby towns.
It appears that hardly a grave remains in Luristan which has
not been robbed by local inhabitants. Little is left for the spade of
the experienced archaeologist. For lack of new sites in Luristan
the scene of digging has shifted largely to other parts of Iran. As
described elsewhere in these pages, many objects have been found
in Amlash, an area directly south of the Caspian Sea.
Many Luristan bells are of the crotal type, both spherical and
ovoid in form; some are distinctly pear-shaped. Within their
cage-like bodies roll one, two, and occasionally three spherical
metal pellets. Those pellets are sometimes of bronze, but usually
of iron. Many bell founders, in other lands as well as Luristan,
placed iron rather than bronze pellets in crotal-type bells and iron
clappers in open-mouthed bells in order to obtain livelier ringing
sounds. Bells have frequently been found empty, their iron pellets
or clappers having rusted away in damp soil. The iron clappers of
cup-shaped bells often drop out when buried, though in some cases
corroded fragments are found adhering to the inside of a bell. All
the bells were cast by the *cire perdue*, or lost-wax, method, a way
of metal founding used to this day in parts of Asia and Africa,
and described in detail in this book in connection with Mexican
copper bells. This method, used extensively in the Western
Hemisphere in the pre-Columbian era, reached its apogee in the
fabrication of gold crotal-type bells by the Mixtecs of Mexico in
the 12th century A.D. In Europe, the finest examples of bells thus
cast were of bronze and of the swinging-clapper variety. Many
were created by famous artisans during the 15th and 16th cen-

Figure 59. Bronze chain with horse bells. Luristan, Iran. Circa 9th century B.C. Length 73.7 cm. (29 in.). Patina light green.

Figure 60. Bronze bell. Luristan, Iran. 10th–9th century B.C. Height 10.5 cm. (4⅛ in.). Patina dark green.

Figure 61. Bronze bell. Luristan, Iran. 9th–8th century B.C. Height 8.9 cm. (3½ in.). Patina light green.

turies. Many metalsmiths traveled the caravan routes, and the shapes and artistic qualities of the bells which they cast influenced the forms of bells cast in far-distant lands.

The bronze chain holding eight cup-shaped bells in Figure 59 may have adorned a Luristan war-horse. Often, however, a single bell of the crotal type hung on a chain at the steed's neck. A careful look at Figure 66 reveals a small hole quite close to the bottom. It was caused by a slight explosion which occurred during the casting of the bell, when steam formed due to dampness in the clay mold. Figures 62–70 represent pomegranates, and the characteristic calyx of a pomegranate appears at the bottom of each. Their ribs vary in number from three to thirteen. None has five. Most have six or eight. The ribs of several bells are twofold, as, for example, those in Figures 62 and 63.

None of the three bronze horse bells in Figures 71–73 was cast with a calyx. Each contains a pellet.

Smaller bells of the swinging-clapper type often decorated the collars and bridles of horses (Figures 74 and 75). The bell in Figure 74 is topped by a representation of the forequarters of two horses, joined back to back. A fragment of the clapper's stem still adheres to the suspension bar. The bell in Figure 75, of high copper content, shows two horse's heads in profile facing in opposite directions. The clapper is missing. Only the ends of the suspension bar remain and protrude slightly from the bell's outside surface. Small bells of the crotal type such as those in Figures 76–88 served the same purpose. The ribs of the bell shown in Figure 60 display deep diagonal markings.

Bells sometimes were crowned with the forms of birds and animals, such as the rams in Plate 12 (p. 85), the cocks and ducks in Plate 13 (pp. 88–89), and the ram and goats in Figures 61 and 60. Many of the crotal-type bells, both large and small, have the form of a pomegranate. Since ancient times the pomegranate, a fruit rich in seeds and widely grown throughout Asia and Asia Minor, has been regarded as a symbol of abundance and fecundity. Because bells traditionally were believed to be endowed with the power to protect against harm and all kinds of evil and to bring good fortune, including military success, it is not surprising that they were cast in the form of pomegranates. The wearing of bells became particularly widespread in those lands where periodic

60

61

Figures 62–70. Bronze horse bells.
Luristan, Iran. 9th–8th century B.C.
Figure 66: height 9.5 cm. (3⅝ in.).
Patina dark brown,

Plate 12. (p. 85). Bronze bell. Luristan,
Iran. 9th–8th century B.C. *Height 7.6*
cm. (3 in.), diameter 5.1 cm. (2 in.).
Patina mottled brown and green.

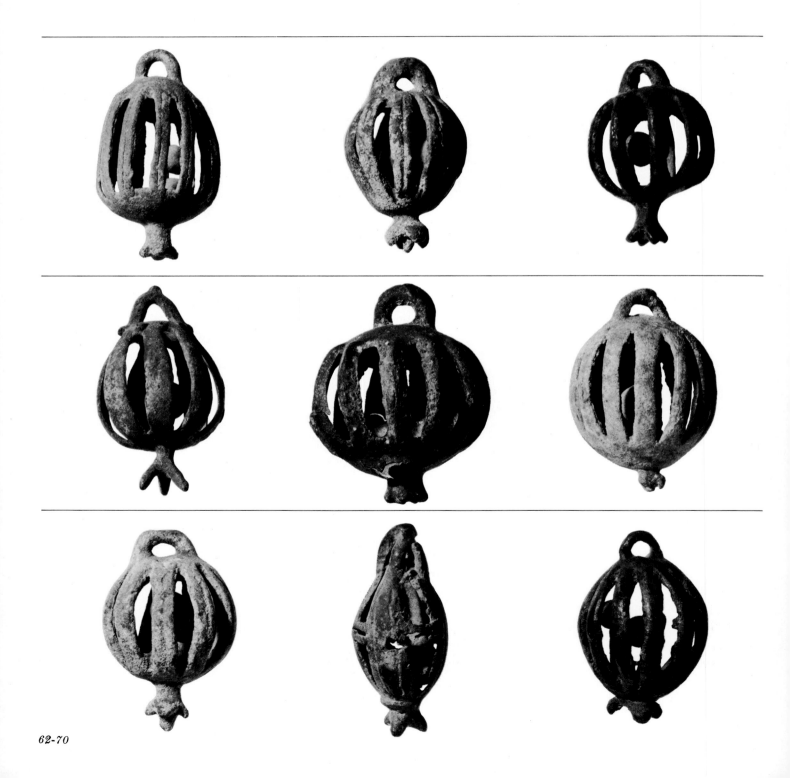

62-70

Figures 71–73. Bronze horse bells. Luristan, Iran. 9th–8th century B.C. *71: height 7.6 cm. (3 in.). Patina dark green. 72: height 7.9 cm. (3⅛ in.). Patina light green. 73: height 7 cm. (2¾ in.). Patina dark green.*

Figures 74 and 75. Bronze horse-bridle bells. Luristan, Iran. 9th–8th century B.C. *74: height 4.1 cm. (1⅝ in.), diameter 3.3 cm. (1 5/16 in.). Patina dark green. 75: height 3.7 cm. (1 7/16 in.), diameter 2.9 cm. (1⅛ in.). Patina light green.*

71-73

74-75

Figures 76–87. Bronze horse-bridle bells. Luristan, Iran. 9th–8th century B.C. *Figure 76: height 3.6 cm. (1⁷⁄₁₆ in.). Patina light green.*

Plate 13 (pp. 88–89). Bronze bells. Luristan, Iran. Circa 8th century B.C. *Left: height 10.1 cm. (4 in.). Patina grayish green. Right: height 8.2 cm. (3¼ in.). Patina dark green.*

76-79

80-83

84-87

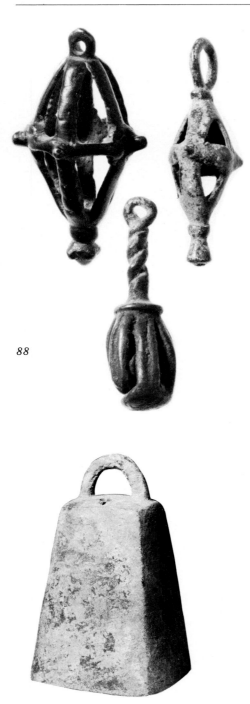

88

89

drought and resulting famine threatened not only the lives of the inhabitants but also their herds, flocks, and precious horses. Small bells of pomegranate form were frequently worn as talismans by humans, while those of larger size were hung at the necks of horses and other domesticated animals. Groups of small bells often decorated horses' bridles.

In designing their bells, many Luristan bell casters adhered closely to the form of a pomegranate, showing a representation of the multi-pointed calyx at the bottom of the fruit. At its top was cast the bell's suspension ring. The multitudinous seeds of the fruit were inadequately represented by but one or two and occasionally three pellets which rolled about inside the bell. Certain craftsmen, however, deviated both from the natural shape and size of a pomegranate and from the shape and size of the calyx. Often they omitted the calyx entirely. Some gave an extremely stylized form to such bells, even to the point of producing geometric designs. A striking example is the bell in the upper left-hand corner of Figure 88. Its six ribs are angular and are connected with one another at their midsections by crossbars, punctuated by small nodes. It is interesting to note, however, that the bottom of the bell carries the characteristic calyx of a pomegranate. In Figure 89 is a four-sided bell with two holes in its crown, where the swinging clapper, now missing, was suspended. The bell still has a fine ring.

The ovoid bronze chariot bell in Plate 14 (pp. 92–93) is a fine specimen of casting by the conventional *cire perdue* method. Like the bells from Susa shown in Figure 40, this bell has been cast with a suspension ring at each end. The rings are placed at right angles to each other. The bell was probably hung on thongs or ropes across the front of the chariot box. The bell is of intricate openwork design and is divided vertically in the middle by a narrow and slightly convex band. The two halves carry almost identical patterns made up of a series of straight and crescent-shaped convex bars. Each half also carries four swastikas. The swastika, a mystic symbol of ancient origin, is depicted upon many objects, both religious and profane, and is found not only in the Asiatic but also in North American areas. The word "swastika" is derived from Sanskrit and means "good luck" or "well-being." Of the eight swastikas on the bell, six have their crampons directed in the ancient,

94

Figures 91 and 92. Bronze horse bells. Lake Urmia, Iran. Circa 500–300 B.C. 91: height 7 cm. (2¾ in.), diameter 5.1 cm. (2 in.). Patina light green. 92: height 6.4 cm. (2½ in.), diameter 4.5 cm. (1¾ in.). Patina dark green.

counterclockwise manner, whereas two go clockwise in the style of the emblem of Nazi Germany, officially adopted in 1935.

The bell contains two metal pellets.

The 9th century B.C. Luristan horse bell in Figure 90 is suspended from an eighty-six-link bronze chain composed of four sections held together by three rings. The bell has eight ribs, each of which is deeply incised down the center with a single line. At the bottom of the bell are five small round holes arranged in a circle. The suspension ring was created by casting the forequarters of two stylized bearded ibexes facing in opposite directions. It has a single pellet.

The Environs of Lake Urmia, Iran

West of the southern part of the Caspian Sea in northwestern Iran, and not far from Iran's Turkish and Iraqi borders, lies Lake Urmia. Nearby in a wide, fertile plain called Solduz and dotting the landscape all about are the large and small mounds (tepes) of many ancient buried towns and villages. Within them, layer upon layer, in some cases at fifth millennium B.C. level, lie rubble, ashes, and worldly goods tempting the spade of both the archaeologist and the illicit digger. The bell shown in Figure 91 was reportedly found in the environs of the lake.

Extensive excavations at late 9th century B.C. level carried out at Hasanlu, just to the south, have resulted in many important finds—pottery, carved ivories, jewelry, weapons, charred bits of textiles, and the bones of humans as well as those of both domestic and wild animals.

Tribal warfare marked the early history of nearly all of Asia Minor, and the area around Lake Urmia was no exception. Here and elsewhere, the horses of a particular tribe wore bells of identical form which produced identical sounds. One way of accomplishing this was by casting each bell with a vertical slit of predetermined length. The slit ran directly up the mantle from the bell's mouth, as shown by the bell in Figure 91. A similar effect was obtained by casting bells all of the same form and possessing apertures equal in number and of identical geometric shape, generally triangular, as in the bell in Figure 92.

Definite proof of both of these procedures has been provided by the excavation of graves in many tribal cemeteries, where

91

Plate 15 (pp. 96–97). Bronze horse bells. Babylon, Iraq. Sargon Period, circa 700 B.C. Left: height 7.6 cm. (2¾ in.), diameter 5.1 cm. (2 in.). Patina dark green. Right: height 8.3 cm. (3¼ in.), diameter 6.4 cm. (2½ in.). Patina light green with incrustation.

all the horse bells unearthed were found to be alike. Thus when a troop of horsemen was heard approaching, the inhabitants of a village knew from the distinctive sound of the bells whether it was friend or foe.

The bell in Figure 91 has a slightly granulated surface. Its three-quarter-round suspension ring rises from a circular platform pierced off-center by a small hole. There is an indication of a second hole alongside, now filled by corrosion. The clapper is missing. A very narrow flange runs around the bell's mouth.

The bell in Figure 92 is cone-shaped. Originally a thin bar cast with the bell stretched across the open crown to support a clapper. Both bar and clapper are now missing. Around the lower half of the mantle are four equidistant, triangular apertures, their apexes pointing upward.

92

Babylonia

During a period spanning more than fifty centuries, civilizations, both prehistoric and historic, flourished and withered in the region watered by the Tigris and Euphrates rivers. Known in comparatively modern times as Mesopotamia, it now comprises the major part of the Republic of Iraq. There, history records the rise and fall of mighty kingdoms, powerful city-states, and many communities of lesser importance. Periods of peace, sometimes very brief, were broken by predatory raids and wars of varying duration. Invasions from abroad remained a constant threat. Its northern territory and the valley of the Tigris long comprised the Kingdom of Assyria; the southern area situated between the two rivers was dominated by the Kingdom of Babylonia, its capital at Babylon.

The bronze horse bells in Plate 15 (pp. 96–97), were obtained originally by purchase at Ur. They reportedly were found together with other objects dating from the reign of Sargon II, who was King of Assyria from 722 until his death in 705 B.C. Five years before, he had defeated King Merodach-baladan, had captured Babylon, and had subjugated all of Babylonia. The bell at the left has a plain and comparatively smooth surface with an arched suspension ring cast as part of the bell. A hole in the bell's crown originally held the split prongs of the clapper; the clapper is missing. The bell at the right has a rough surface due to corrosion. A

Figure 93. Bronze bell. Babylon, Iraq. 9th–8th century B.C. Height 4.7 cm. (1⅞ in.), diameter 2.7 cm. (1¹⁄₁₆ in.). Patina light green, heavily incrusted with soil. Courtesy of the Trustees of The British Museum, London.

narrow flange runs around its mouth. The clapper is missing, but
two small fragments of its pronged upper end fill the hole in the
bell's crown. A slit runs three quarters of the way up the mantle of
each bell.

The bell in Figure 93 was discovered in 1880 in the environs of
the ancient site of Babylon during excavations directed by the
renowned Chaldean archaeologist Hormuzd Rassam (1826–1910).

Nimrud

On the left bank of the Tigris stood Nimrud, for years the
military capital of the Assyrians. Nimrud, called Calah in the
Bible, ranked with Nineveh, Assur, and Khorsabad as one of the
four greatest cities of the Assyrian Empire. To the Assyrians it
was known as Kalhu. In 883 B.C., under King Ashurnasirpal II,
a name meaning "Ashur protects a son" (reigned 883–859 B.C.),
regarded as the most despotic and cruel of Assyrian rulers,
Nimrud became the capital of the Empire. It remained so until
shortly before the close of the 8th century B.C., when King
Sargon II shortly before his death in battle established a new
capital at Khorsabad, fifteen miles (twenty-four kilometers)
northeast of Nineveh.

At the great mound at Nimrud the celebrated English archaeologist Sir Austen Henry Layard, between 1845 and 1857,
excavated part of Ashurnasirpal's Northwest Palace, one of the
finest and best-preserved of all known Assyrian royal monuments.
His efforts brought to light many excellent large-scale bas-reliefs
in limestone which decorated the mud-brick walls and doorways
of the royal buildings. Some one hundred years later, two other
distinguished archaeologists, Sir Max E. L. Mallowan, who
directed excavations at Nimrud from 1949 to 1958, and his
successor, David Oates, who headed the work from 1958 to
1962, received worldwide acclaim when they made important
architectural discoveries and unearthed a remarkable group of
carved ivories.

A characteristic of some of the larger horse bells discovered
at Nimrud is that they were cast with suspension rings. An
example is seen in Figure 94. The clapper is missing, but careful
examination reveals that it originally was suspended from a loop
made from a thin wire which had been placed within the mold
before the metal was poured. In this case, the loop became

102

Figures 96–101. Bronze bells. Nimrud, Assyria. Assyrian, 9th–8th century B.C. 96: height 5 cm. (1³¹⁄₃₂ in.), diameter 3.2 cm. (1¼ in.). Patina mottled light brown and light green. 97: height 5.5 cm. (2³⁄₁₆ in.), diameter 2.3 cm. (⅞ in.). Patina mottled light brown and dark green. 98: height 5 cm. (1³¹⁄₃₂ in.), diameter 3.5 cm. (1⅜ in.). Patina mottled light brown and dark green. 99: height 5.2 cm. (2¹⁄₁₆ in.), diameter 3.5 cm. (1⅜ in.). Patina mottled light brown and light green. 100: height

5.4 cm. (2⅛ in.), diameter 3.4 cm. (1⅜ in.). Patina mottled light brown and dark green. 101: height 5.1 cm. (2 in.), diameter 3.5 cm. (1⅜ in.). Patina mottled light brown and dark green. Courtesy of the Trustees of The British Museum, London.

96-98

99-101

Figures 102–107. Bronze bells. Nimrud, Assyria. Assyrian, 9th–8th century B.C. 102: height 5.5 cm. (2³⁄₁₆ in.), diameter 3.4 cm. (1³⁄₈ in.). Patina light brown flecked with light green. 103: height 4.9 cm. (1¹⁵⁄₁₆ in.), diameter 3.3 cm. (1⁵⁄₁₆ in.). Patina light brown flecked with light green. 104: height 5 cm. (1³¹⁄₃₂ in.), diameter 3.4 cm. (1³⁄₈ in.). Patina light green. 105: height 5.1 cm. (2 in.), diameter 3.5 cm. (1³⁄₈ in.). Patina dark brown flecked with light green. 106: height 4.9 cm. (1¹⁵⁄₁₆ in.), diameter 3.2 cm. (1¼ in.). Patina light brown after cleaning. 107: height 5 cm. (1³¹⁄₃₂ in.), diameter 3.4 cm. (1³⁄₈ in.). Patina mottled dark brown and dark green. Courtesy of the Trustees of The British Museum, London.

102-104

105-107

Figure 108. Bronze bell. Nimrud, Assyria. Assyrian, 9th–8th century B.C. Height 5.1 cm. (2 in.), diameter 3.3 cm. (1⁵⁄₁₆ in.). Patina mottled light green and dark brown. Courtesy of the Trustees of The British Museum, London.

108

corroded and broke off, leaving only the tips of the wire protruding inside the bell's crown.

Resembling this bell in its general form is the one seen hanging at the horse's neck on the limestone bas-relief in Figure 95, removed from the Southwest Palace of Tiglath-pileser III (reigned 744–727 B.C.) at Nimrud.

Figures 96–101 show six smaller bronze horse bells excavated at Nimrud by Layard between 1848 and 1851. The crown of each is open at the top and is spanned by a suspension arch. Their clappers originally hung from horizontal round bars riveted within the upper parts of the crown of the bells. However, only the two bells in Figures 99 and 101 still retain their bars. Their clappers are missing.

Shown in Figure 108 is a horse bell from Nimrud which still retains its long clapper, the end of which is clearly visible.

The six horse bells in Figures 102–107 were also found at Nimrud by Layard. They are similar in shape to those in Figures 96–101 except that atop each arch and cast with it is a round ring for suspension. This arrangement appears to be unique and permitted the bells to swing more freely from the horses' collars. These bells have also lost their clappers, and only a few still possess their bars.

Nineveh It is characteristic of Assyrian bells that many of the clappers are quite long, extending well below the mouth, as those seen on the war-horses in Figure 109. The photograph reveals a 7th century B.C. bas-relief fragment, discovered in the mound of Kuyunjik at Nineveh during the excavation of part of the palace of Ashurbanipal, a name meaning "Ashur creates a son" (reigned 668–627 B.C.), by the French architect and archaeologist Victor Place (1818–75). The scene depicts Assyrian troops in combat against the Elamites. Portrayed are two war chariots drawn by stallions yoked in pairs, though only those steeds to the right of the chariot draw poles are fully visible. As the vehicles advance, their drivers and bowmen are protected by shield bearers standing directly behind them. Ahead of the lower chariot is the figure of an archer who is in full battle gear and is mounted upon a beautifully caparisoned stallion wearing a bell. In combat, the archer expected the sound of the bell, in addition to his battle cry,

to help confuse and panic the enemy. Upon the bas-relief the archer is shown riding in the customary manner of the period—that is, with saddlecloth but without saddle, stirrups, or spurs. This gave him freedom of movement and permitted him to dismount quickly and fight afoot with his short sword; but it also limited his ability to control his steed or even quicken its pace. At times, the Assyrians attempted to offset this disadvantage by having a mounted attendant lead the archer's horse and protect him with a shield. But this obviously had other disadvantages and the plight of the mounted archer was not relieved until stirrups were introduced by the Scythians. It is said that the use of stirrups by the Franks in the Middle Ages accounted in large measure for the overwhelming success of their cavalry in western Europe.

Figure 110 shows an exquisite limestone bas-relief detail, removed from the walls of Ashurbanipal's palace. It depicts the king wearing his crown and standing in the box of his chariot. He faces backward and, about to leave on a lion hunt, is being handed a bow. Two attendants standing behind him are being given spears, while three others are in the act of harnessing a pair of stallions wearing collars decorated with bells.

On the bas-relief depicted in Figure 111, Ashurbanipal is seen without his royal headdress; instead, he wears an embroidered band to hold his flowing locks in place. He rides to the hunt on a lavishly equipped stallion from whose embossed leather collar hangs a single bronze bell. A bell identical in form, unearthed at Nineveh, is depicted in Figure 112. Its long clapper is missing, but a portion of the suspension bar in a very corroded condition still remains within the bell. Riding closely behind the monarch are both his arrow bearer and his spear bearer, whose mounts also have leather collars with bells.

In Figure 113 a spearman advances on foot, leading two rider-less stallions. On the lower edge of the collar worn by the stallion in the foreground is a row of four small bronze bells of graduated size. Four similar bells, all found at Nineveh, have been assembled and are shown in Figures 114–117. The first three in the group were discovered between 1927 and 1932 during excavations directed by the British Assyriologist R. Campbell Thompson. The fourth was unearthed in 1880 by Hormuzd Rassam.

Figure 109. Bas-relief fragment, Palace of King Ashurbanipal. Assyrian Troops in combat against the Elamites. Nineveh, Assyria. Height 1.1 m. (43⁵⁄₁₆ in.). Courtesy of the Musée du Louvre, Paris.

Figure 110. Detail, limestone bas-relief, Palace of King Ashurbanipal. The King stands in his chariot, drawn by two stallions wearing bells. Nineveh, Assyria. Courtesy of the Trustees of The British Museum, London.

109

110

108

111

112

Figure 113. Detail, limestone bas-relief, Palace of King Ashurbanipal. Nineveh, Assyria. Courtesy of the Trustees of The British Museum, London.

Figures 114–117. Bronze bells. Nineveh, Assyria. Assyrian, 9th–8th century B.C. 114: height 3.6 cm. (1 7/16 in.), diameter 2.6 cm. (1 in.). Patina greenish gray, incrusted with soil. 115: height 3.2 cm. (1 1/4 in.), diameter 2.1 cm. (13/16 in.). Patina light green, incrusted with soil. 116: height 2.9 cm. (1 1/8 in.), diameter 2.1 cm. (13/16 in.). Patina light green. 117: height 2.8 cm. (1 3/32 in.), diameter 1.8 cm. (11/16 in.). Patina greenish gray. Courtesy of the Trustees of The British Museum, London.

113

114-117

Bells on horses ridden to the hunt served several purposes:
to embellish the collars, as talismans, and to frighten enraged
beasts bent on attacking both horse and rider.

118

119

Urartu First mention of Urartu occurs in early Assyrian accounts from
the first half of the 9th century B.C., when, in the environs of Lake
Van, many small tribes began to consolidate under one ruler. The
new and growing state of Urartu emerged at a time when the
Middle East was witnessing the decline of the mighty kingdoms
of Egypt and Babylon and had seen the disappearance of the
extensive empire of the Hittites. As Urartu expanded northward
to the Araxes River and eastward to Lake Urmia, its southern
borders began to meet aggressive attacks from Assyria. From
that time until the destruction of Nineveh in 612 B.C. at the hands
of the Babylonians, the Medes, and certain nomadic tribes,
including Scythians, the histories of the two countries were to be
closely related, primarily through warfare. A partial record of
that is vividly preserved on some of the bronze reliefs which
ornamented a pair of wooden gates, known as the Balawat Gates,
erected at the entrance of the palace of Shalmaneser III, King of
Assyria from 860 to 825 B.C. These gates derived their name from
the place of their discovery, a small mound, Tell Balawat, some
fifteen miles (twenty-four kilometers) from Mosul, Iraq. A band
on one of the bronze reliefs portrays Urartians with yokes at
their necks being led away into Assyrian captivity; another band
shows naked bodies impaled. Some of the bronze reliefs of the
Balawat Gates are now among the treasures of The British
Museum; the others are owned by the Iraq Museum in Baghdad.
In the middle of the 19th century, when archaeological expeditions, particularly from England and France, were initiating
scientific excavations in Assyria and Babylonia, native treasure
hunters in Urartu, unmolested, were vigorously working
digs and bringing forth valuable material, much of which
ultimately reached the important museums of Europe. In 1859,
among antiquities acquired by The State Hermitage Museum in
Leningrad were three bronze horse bells, illustrated in Figures
118–120. They had been found unexpectedly when some Kurds of
the Jalali tribe, camping upon a rocky promontory in Iranian
territory overlooking the Araxes River not far from the Cossack

Figures 118–120. Bronze bells. Urartu (Eastern Turkey). 8th century B.C. 118: height 10 cm. (3¹⁵⁄₁₆ in.), diameter 7.9 cm. (3⅛ in.). Patina dark brown. 119: height 10.8 cm. (4¼ in.), diameter 7.6 cm. (3 in.). Patina dark brown. 120: height 10.8 cm. (4¼ in.), diameter 7 cm. (2¾ in.). Patina dark brown. Courtesy of The State Hermitage Museum, Leningrad.

military post of Alishar, discovered the entrance to a cave. Exploration of the cave disclosed a number of ancient Urartian burial chambers, in one of which were the bells, together with two harness mounts and what appeared to be a fragment of a vessel or a bracelet; unquestionably, these had been brought there as funerary gifts.

The body of the bell in Figure 119 is divided vertically into eight equal-sized panels. The crown, which is composed of five alternating smooth and ribbed circles, is surmounted by a suspension ring resting upon a domed platform of inverted lotus petals. Two rectangular apertures appear opposite one another near the center of the bell's waist. The bell in Figure 118 is cup-shaped and has a smooth surface. A bow-shaped suspension loop stretches gracefully across its crown. At one spot, just above the lip of the bell, are two identical symbols, which might be identified as snake's mouths with protruding tongues. The clappers of both of these bells are missing.

In Figure 120 is a third bronze horse bell found in the Alishar hoard. This bell resembles somewhat a one-story Chinese pagoda. Each of the eight sides of its midsection is perforated by a rectangular aperture. The crown and shoulder of the bell are plain; they support a slightly raised platform and suspension ring cast with the bell. Directly below a ridged section which separates the shoulder from the waist is a legend inscribed in cuneiform characters running completely around the bell. Professor A. Waimann, Keeper of the Oriental Department of the State Hermitage Museum at Leningrad, has transliterated it as follows: "ar-gi-iŝ-ti ú-ri-iŝ-ḫi." It is believed that the name "ar-gi-iŝ-ti" refers to Argishti I (reigned 789–766 B.C.), son of Menua.

When the author noticed a drawing of the bell with its cuneiform inscription in B. B. Piotrovskii's book *Urartu*, he recalled that in his own collection was a horse bell of somewhat similar form, which was heavily incrusted. Examination of the bell under a magnifying glass disclosed several cuneiform characters. At the suggestion of Dr. Vaughn E. Crawford, Curator in Charge, Department of Ancient Near Eastern Art at The Metropolitan Museum of Art, New York, the narrow section around the bell

120

Figures 121 and 122. Bronze bell. Urartu (Eastern Turkey). 8th century B.C. 121: before cleaning. 122: after cleaning. Height 8.6 cm. (3⅜ in.), diameter 5.7 cm. (2¼ in.). Patina very light green.

which had given evidence of carrying an inscription was cleaned in the Museum's laboratory. The procedure revealed the same cuneiform inscription which appears on the Hermitage bell: "ar-gi-iš-ti ú-ri-iš-ḫi." It is noteworthy that the cuneiform inscriptions on both the Hermitage bell and the author's bell are identical with the one found upon a bronze buckle from an excavation made in 1950 at Karmir Blur, Armenian S.S.R., and recorded by Friedrich Wilhelm König in his *Handbuch die Chaldischen Inschriften* (*Handbook of Chaldean Inscriptions*). König translated the cuneiform inscription into German as follows: "*Der dem Argisti eigenen Waffen-*(*oder Toten*) *Kammer zugehörig*," meaning: "Which belongs to Argishti's own armory (or mortuary)." The bell in the author's collection, pictured in Figures 121 and 122 before and after cleaning, differs from the Hermitage bell in that it is in the shape of a two-story rather than a one-story pagoda. It has sixteen rectangular apertures. Moreover, its crown and shoulder, instead of having a plain, smooth surface like that of the Hermitage bell, are in the form of an inverted lotus flower with long narrow petals standing out in high relief. The inverted-lotus-petal motif in low relief made its appearance later in variegated forms on the crowns of many religious bells, particularly altar bells, throughout Tibet, China, Mongolia, and Japan, following the spread of Buddhism from India. The bell's clapper is missing, but a four-sided horizontal bar for its suspension is firmly riveted inside. This bell, the provenance of which is unknown, was acquired from an antiquarian in New York.

The Caucasus

Certain details of design distinguish the bronze bells excavated in the Russian Caucasus, between the Black and Caspian seas, from those found in nearby lands. These bells are identified with several cultures of Ural-Altaic origin during three ages: the Late Bronze Age, the transitional period between it and the First Iron Age, and the First Iron Age itself. These cultures were linked to a people known as the Tchoudes and, at one time, apparently to the Scythians.

Some of the most important archaeological discoveries relating to these periods were made toward the end of the 19th century in the necropolis of Verkhnii Koban, a small Ossetian village

Figure 123. Bronze bells on chain. Verkhnii Koban, Georgian S.S.R. Ural-Altaic Culture, 11th–10th century B.C. Each bell: height 4.2 cm. (1⅝ in.), diameter 2.8 cm. (1⅛ in.). Patina light green. Courtesy of the Musée des Antiquités Nationales, Château de Saint-Germain-en-Laye (Yvelines), France.

123

situated at an altitude of about 2,400 feet, approximately twenty-two miles (thirty-five kilometers) southwest of Ordzhonikidze. Though the inhabitants of Verkhnii Koban knew that a necropolis had existed in the area, there was no external indication of its exact location until about 1869, when a flood washed away part of the hillside in what is known as the Upper Village and exposed a number of graves. Sporadic digging by local inhabitants seeking treasure was followed by scientific work on the part of two Russian archaeologists, Filimonov and Antonowitch, the former reaching the site in 1877. It has been recorded that he discovered many objects, including four small bells. In 1879 a French archaeologist, Ernest Chantre, came to study the necropolis and returned to dig there in 1881. Among the objects he unearthed were two crotal-type bells attached to the ends of a bronze chain composed of seventy-five links (Figure 123). Both bells are identical in size and are attached to the chain by thin wire rings. Each bell has three small triangular apertures in its waist as well as three in its bottom. One of the bells contained a single pellet; the other was found to be empty. The bronze bell in Figure 124 is from the same cemetery. Its clapper is missing. An unusual and decorative touch is added by the narrow longitudinal welts which stand out in relief on the bell's outer surface. These were probably made by the bell founder, who allowed molten wax to drip down and harden on the smooth surface of the model before the bell was cast by the prevailing lost-wax method. The suspension loop, cast as part of the bell, is worn very thin at the top, almost to the point of breaking.

Opinions of archaeologists have differed greatly in attributing dates to the objects discovered at Verkhnii Koban, especially since many burials were superimposed one upon the other and, in some cases, objects of iron were found alongside bronze ones. Claude F. A. Schaeffer has ascribed the approximate date of 1250 B.C. to bells and other objects discovered there. A. M. Tallgren dated them between 1300 and 900 B.C., a period that antedates the dates ascribed to the Scythian finds at Kazbek. R. Virchow believed the finds at Verkhnii Koban belong to the beginning of the Iron Age and placed them at 1100 to 900 B.C.

The bell depicted in Figure 125 was found in an ancient necropolis

Figure 124. Bronze bell. Verkhnii Koban, Georgian S.S.R. Ural-Altaic Culture, 11th–10th century B.C. *Height 7 cm. (2¾ in.), diameter 3.8 cm. (1½ in.). Patina pale bluish green. Courtesy of the Musée des Antiquités Nationales, Château de Saint-Germain-en-Laye (Yvelines), France.*

Figure 125. Bronze bell. Gori, Georgian S.S.R. Ural-Altaic Culture, first millennium B.C. *Height 6.3 cm. (2½ in.), diameter 4.2 cm. (1⅝ in.). Patina light green. Courtesy of the Musée des Antiquités Nationales, Château de Saint-Germain-en-Laye (Yvelines), France.*

124   125

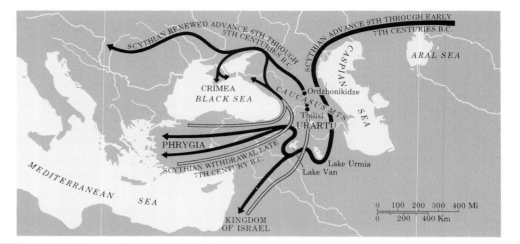

at Gori, a town northwest of Tbilisi (Tiflis) in the north central part of the Georgian S.S.R., close to the Caucasus. Noteworthy is the bell's very plain, smooth surface. A slit in the bell runs more than halfway up its mantle. The clapper is missing.

The Scythians and Their Migrations

The Scythians in many ways have been an enigma to archaeologists and historians alike. The consensus, however, is that their place of origin was somewhere in the East. An intrepid, warlike, illiterate, nomadic people, entirely dependent upon their horses in constant predatory activities and battles, they made their way westward, subduing all who stood in their path.

In their wanderings during the 9th–early 7th centuries B.C. they pressed westward over vast stretches of Asia; crossed the Caucasus and advanced in Asia Minor as far west as Phrygia and as far south as the Kingdom of Israel. Following their defeat in 625 B.C. at the hands of Cyaxeres (653–585 B.C.), King of the Medes, they withdrew in a northerly move, and passing through Urartu, they recrossed the Caucasus. Many settled in the area between Tbilisi (Tiflis) and Ordzhonikidze. Thence they moved northwest, occupying land in the Kuban River District, later entering the Crimea and other areas along the shores of the Sea of Azov. From there they moved in a northerly direction to the territory between the Bug and Dnieper rivers. From what is now the heart of the Ukraine they continued on into the broad Carpathian Basin. Unlike the graves of the Avars, which have yielded a comparatively limited amount of goods, those of the Scythians have contained much of great intrinsic value and of the highest artistic quality. Many unusual and beautiful objects of gold, masterpieces created by both Greek and Scythian craftsmen, have been found in Scythian graves. The discoveries have amply rewarded the efforts of dedicated Russian archaeologists.

The Scythians in the Caucasus

An important site of Scythian treasure was the hamlet of Kazbek, which lies on the right bank of the river Terek, along the route from Tbilisi to Ordzhonikidze. In 1871, workmen leveling a military road there suddenly came upon a cache of varied objects of gold, silver, bronze, and iron. It is known as the Kazbek

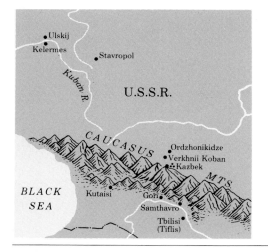

Treasure. In 1877, G. D. Filimonov, after having dug at
Verkhnii Koban, began work at Kazbek. In a trench eighteen
feet deep, which he dug in the courtyard of a house near the road
where the initial find was made, Filimonov found the bronze
memorial shown in Figure 126. It is interesting to compare this
memorial of the 6th to 5th century B.C. with the Roman one of the
1st century A.D. unearthed in Orange, France, and shown in
Figure 231.

The Kazbek piece is comprised of nine stylized bull's heads,
equally divided into three groups, with the heads superimposed
one upon the other. Most of the horns are intact, but some of
the ears appear to have been broken off and lost. Bull's
horns as religious symbols are found in a number of ancient
Near Eastern cultures, even as early as the one at Catal Hayuk,
Anatolia, about 6500 B.C. At the top of the piece, standing astride
the uppermost horns, is a male figure completely nude except for
boots. The Finnish archaeologist A. M. Tallgren has identified
the figure as Teshub, a Hittite deity, known as the Weather God
and, sometimes, as the Storm God. He is shown brandishing in his
right hand what appears to be a mallet, with which he would
presumably strike a blow to create a peal of thunder and a bolt of
lightning. The mouths of the three bull's heads at the bottom of
the memorial have been cast in the form of rings. From these hang
three bronze bells, all with slits in their mantles. The slits in two
of them are visible in the photograph. The bells' clappers are
missing. They were of the variety which were split at the top to
form two thin prongs. Originally, after being passed through the
holes in the bells' crowns, the prongs were bent down in opposite
directions. In the crown of the bell at the right a few corroded
fragments from the top of its clapper still adhere.

The bronze pole-top in Plate 16 is of the early 5th century B.C.
and was excavated in 1909 from barrow No. 2 at Ulskij in the
Kuban River District by N. G. Weselovskij. On each side of its
flat surfaces are identical designs which show the outline of a
bird's head with large curved beak, conveyed by a series of
concentric lines. At the back of the bird's neck a human eye is
depicted in high relief. Just forward of it is the recumbent form
of a mountain goat, head turned backwards and legs folded. A

**The Scythians in the Kuban
River District, U.S.S.R.**

Figure 126. Bronze memorial with bells. Kazbek, Georgian S.S.R. Scythian, circa 6th–5th century B.C. Memorial: overall length 19.7 cm. (7¾ in.), width 10.2 cm. (4 in.). Patina dark and light brown. Bells: height 6.4 cm. (2½ in.), diameter 3.5 cm. (1⅜ in.). Patina light green. Courtesy of The State Historical Museum, Moscow.

Plate 16 (p. 119). Bronze pole-top bells. Ulskij, Kuban River District, U.S.S.R. Scythian, early 5th century B.C. Height 26.5 cm. (10⅞ in.). Patina greenish brown. Courtesy of The State Hermitage Museum, Leningrad.

Figure 127. Bronze pole-top bell. Kelermes, Kuban River Basin, U.S.S.R. Scythian, 6th century B.C. Height 31 cm. (12³⁄₁₆ in.). Patina light green. Courtesy of The State Hermitage Museum, Leningrad.

Figure 128. Bronze pole-top bell. Ulskij, Kuban River District, U.S.S.R. Scythian, early 5th century B.C. Height 24.2 cm. (9⁹⁄₁₆ in.). Patina dark brown. Courtesy of The State Hermitage Museum, Leningrad.

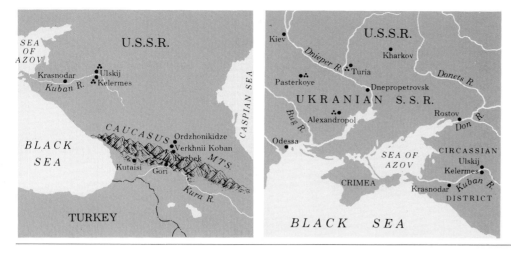

bronze bell of the swinging-clapper type hangs on a half-ring from the eye and another one is similarly suspended from the beak. In this respect, particularly, this pole-top differs from some of the other Scythian pole-tops, such as those shown in Figures 127, 128, and 136, which are themselves bells. At approximately the same level as the lower half-ring is part of a broken half-ring. Undoubtedly, a bell was originally suspended there. The mantle of each bell is split halfway up from the bottom. Riveted near the base of the pole-top's large oval-shaped socket is the head of the pin which formerly held the pole-top firmly to its pole.
Excavating during the same year in barrow No. 2 at Ulskij, N. G. Weselovskij discovered the eight-ribbed bronze pole-top bell shown in Figure 128. It dates from the early 5th century B.C. The bell's cone-shaped body is surmounted by the head of a bull, executed in a realistic manner and cast with sharply defined features. An artistic effect is added by the form of a collar around the bull's neck. Two iron pellets roll within the bell.
The 6th century B.C. pole-top bell in Figure 127 came from barrow No. 3, located south of the town of Kelermes in the Krasnodar region. It was excavated by G. D. Schulz during 1903–04. Within its pear-shaped body are two iron pellets, not visible in the photograph. On top rises a fierce-looking griffin's head with large pointed ears, enormous beak, and bulging eyes. A half-ring, similar to that on the bell in Figure 136, extends from a point just above the bottom of the bell's quadrilateral socket.

The Scythians in the Lower Dnieper River District, Ukrainian S.S.R.

In 1898, V. V. Khvoiko, while carrying out extensive excavations on the Galushchin property near the village of Pastyrskoe in the Circassian District, Ukrainian S.S.R., unearthed forty-two bells from burial mounds (kurgans) of the 4th century B.C. Among them was the Scythian bronze bell pictured in Figure 130. It has a solid mantle which flares broadly at the base. The clapper is missing. Another bell in the find was the Scythian bronze bell shown in Figure 131. Its mantle contains two arrow-shaped apertures pointing upward and lying opposite each other. A bar which runs across the interior of the bell supports an iron clapper.
In 1905 excavations were carried out under the direction of A. A. Bobrinskii at a 5th century B.C. burial mound, No. 459,

Figures 129: bronze bell (B 46–149). Turia, Circassian District, Ukrainian S.S.R. Scythian, 5th century B.C. *Height 6.8 cm. (2¹¹⁄₁₆ in.), diameter 3.5 cm. (1⅜ in.). Patina brown.*

130: bronze bell (B 693). Pastyrskoe, Circassian District, Ukrainian S.S.R. Scythian, 4th century B.C. *Height 5 cm. (1¹⁵⁄₁₆ in.), diameter 3.5 cm. (1⅜ in.). Patina brown.*

131: bronze bell (B 695). Pastyrskoe, Circassian District, Ukrainian S.S.R. Scythian, 4th century B.C. *Height 6.9 cm. (2¾ in.), diameter 4.8 cm. (1⅞ in.). Patina brown. Courtesy of The State Historical Museum of the Ukrainian S.S.R., Kiev.*

129

130

131

near the village of Turia, Circassian District, Ukrainian S.S.R. Among the grave goods unearthed was the Scythian bronze bell portrayed in Figure 129. Its bulbous mantle, which decreases noticeably in diameter at the bell's mouth, has a slit running three quarters of the way up. The clapper is missing.

In 1851 in a large barrow called "Lugovaga Mogila," near Aleksandropol in the Lower Dnieper River District, workers found by chance the early 3rd century B.C. bronze pole-top shown in Figure 133. It is in the shape of a stylized tree with three branches, upon each of which is perched a beautifully executed figure of a bird. The entire object with its large, hollow conical socket appears to have been cast in one piece. The birds at right and left hold cup-shaped bells in their beaks. Corroded fragments of clappers remain in each bell, and bars for clappers are still present in both bells. A hole in the beak of the center bird indicates that at one time a bell was suspended from it. There are two holes two thirds of the way up on opposite sides of the center branch to which decorations may have been attached. Just below that branch is a third hole, choked by corrosion.

The bronze pole-top in Figure 132 also dates from the early 3rd century B.C. It was found by the archaeologist Tereshtchenko during excavations carried out at the aforementioned barrow in 1853. The object is of openwork design and presents in profile the figure of a griffin. Its well-defined features appear on both sides. The animal is enclosed in a rectangular frame, one side of which it grasps with its right front paw. The representation of a griffin on a pole-top carried into battle is most appropriate, since this mythical animal was looked upon as a guard, possessed of a lion's power and an eagle's sight. From the lower section of the frame, two bronze bells of the swinging-clapper variety are suspended by wires. The clappers of both bells are missing, as are also the bars for suspending them. Available for hanging banners or other accessories are two half-rings cast on opposite sides of the pyramid-shaped socket. Just below these are holes through which a nail formerly passed to secure the socket to its pole.

Figure 132. Bronze pole-top with bells. Aleksandropol, Lower Dnieper River District, U.S.S.R. Scythian, early 3rd century B.C. *Height 16.2 cm. (6⅜ in.). Patina greenish brown. Courtesy of The State Hermitage Museum, Leningrad.*

Figure 133. Bronze pole-top with bells. Aleksandropol, Lower Dnieper River District, U.S.S.R. Scythian, early 3rd century B.C. *Height 28.9 cm. (11⅜ in.). Patina dark brown. Courtesy of The State Hermitage Museum, Leningrad.*

132   133

The Scythians in Rumania

In Rumania and Hungary many bronze bells of both the crotal type and those housing swinging clappers have been unearthed. Those of the crotal type discovered in both countries appear to be limited to pole-tops. Almost all of them are substantially conical, the upper parts generally being taken over by the forms of animals. The bronze pole-top bell in Figure 134 was found at Gernyeszeg (Gornesti), Rumania, on the property of Béni Kállay. It may be dated from the end of the 5th century B.C. Running around the base of the outer surface of its beehive-shaped body are double lines. Two more such lines divide the body in its center into two zones. The upper one is pierced by four triangular apertures pointing upward, and the lower one by six slightly larger ones which alternately point upward and downward. Surmounting a discus-shaped base on the body of the bell is what appears to be the figure of a recumbent roe deer, its characteristic short tail turned upward. The socket of the bell is square. No pellet is present.

Toward the close of the 19th century, the late 6th century B.C. bronze pole-top bell shown in Figure 135 was discovered at Somhíd, Rumania, a town not far from the present Hungarian border. It lay without any other finds in the soil on an estate owned by a prince of imperial Austria, Archduke Josef. The bell is of frustum shape, pierced by four triangular apertures with finely chased edges; it is surmounted by the highly stylized figure of what appears to be a roe deer. Slightly more than halfway up its socket is a half-ring suitable for attaching a banner or other form of decoration.

In Figure 136 is a bronze pole-top bell from Gyulafeherver, (Alba Iulia), Rumania, which dates from the end of the 6th to the beginning of the 5th century B.C. It was acquired by the Hungarian National Museum through a dealer; nothing is known of the circumstances in which it was originally found. The body, which is divided into nine flat ribs, angular at their centers, contains two bronze pellets. The bell rests upon an oblong base, above which is a half-ring similar to that on the bell in Figure 135. Cast as part of the bell and extending below it is a long flat rod. There is an oval hole near its lower end through which a rivet originally passed to secure the bell to its pole. When held upside down, the bell appears to have the form of a stylized pomegranate,

Figure 134. Bronze pole-top bell.
Gernyeszeg (Gornesti), Rumania.
Scythian, end of 5th century B.C. Height
21 cm. (8¼ in.). Patina dark brown.
Courtesy of the Hungarian National
Museum, Budapest.

Figure 135. Bronze bell. Somhíd,
Rumania. Scythian, late 6th century
B.C. Height 17.5 cm. (6⅞ in.). Patina
light brown. Courtesy of the Hungarian
National Museum, Budapest.

Figure 136. Bronze pole-top bell.
Gyulafeherver, Rumania. Scythian,
end of 6th–beginning of 5th century
B.C. Height 18.1 cm. (7⅛ in.). Patina
light brown. Courtesy of the Hungarian
National Museum, Budapest.

Figures 137–139. Bronze pole-top bells. Gyöngyös, Hungary. Scythian, second half of 6th century B.C. *137: height 17.7 cm. (7 in.). Patina dark brown. 138: height 15 cm. (5¹⁵⁄₁₆ in.). Patina dark brown. 139: height 17.5 cm. (6⅞ in.). Patina dark brown. Courtesy of the Hungarian National Museum, Budapest.*

137-139

like many Luristan bells. This pomegranate, however, does not have the fruit's characteristic sepals but terminates in the form of a hollow cone.

The three bronze pole-top bells shown in Figures 137–139 date from the second half of the 6th century B.C. They were found at Gyöngyös, Hungary, a small town about forty-one miles (sixty-six kilometers) northeast of Budapest. They were excavated there by the archaeologist Lajos Marton in 1907 and came from a horse-cremation burial within a barrow. Each is surmounted by a figure which appears to be a recumbent roe deer. The upper part of the main body of each bell is pierced by three apertures of swallow-tail shape, equidistant from each other. Directly below each in the lower part of the main body are triangular apertures, their apexes pointing downward. To hold the bell in Figure 137 to a pole is a four-sided iron nail, the head of which rests in the bell's rather small socket. The cylindrical socket of the bell shown in Figure 138 is large enough to admit a pole. The small hole near the base of the socket probably contained a nail to better secure bell and pole. Like the bell in Figure 137, the one in 139 is also fitted with an iron nail, much corroded. Each bell contains a single stone pellet.

In the same mound at Gyöngyös, Lajos Marton discovered a bronze horse bell, two views of which are seen in Figures 140 and 141. The bell, cast in one piece with arched suspension loop, still carries its round iron clapper, split at the upper end to form two prongs. These pass through a hole at the top of the bell, where they are bent in opposite directions. The object's mantle is cracked and, due to damage on both sides of its slit, flares out in a graceful lily-like form. Like the bells in Figures 137–139, this one dates from the second half of the 6th century B.C.

The two bronze frustum-shaped pole-top bells shown in Figures 142 and 143 come from Nagytarcsa, a village a few miles northeast of Budapest. They were found in 1964 by workmen engaged in digging a ditch. The bells date from the second half of the 6th century to the first third of the 5th century B.C. Each supports the figure of a bull. The one in Figure 142 presents a reposing image of that animal. Its eyes protrude; its long, heavy horns sweep gracefully upward to fall just short of forming a ring. In

The Scythians in Hungary

Figures 140 and 141. Bronze bell. Gyöngyös, Hungary. Scythian, second half of 6th century B.C. Height 7.8 cm. (3¹⁄₁₆ in.), diameter 3.8 cm. (1½ in.). Patina light brown. Courtesy of the Hungarian National Museum, Budapest.

Figures 142 and 143. Bronze pole-top bells. Nagytarcsa, Hungary. Scythian, second half of 6th century–first third of 5th century B.C. 142: height 21.3 cm. (8³⁄₈ in.). Patina light brown. 143: height 23.1 cm. (9¹⁄₈ in.). Patina light brown. Courtesy of the Hungarian National Museum, Budapest.

140

141

142

143

Figures 144 and 145. Bronze bell. Nagytarcsa, Hungary. Scythian, late 6th–5th century B.C. Height 9.8 cm. (3⅞ in.), diameter 4.8 cm. (1¹¹⁄₁₆ in.). Patina light brown. Courtesy of the Hungarian National Museum, Budapest.

the body of the bell are three triangular apertures set equidistant to one another. Within the bell is a single iron pellet. Just above the rim of the socket and directly opposite each other are two small holes through which a small round pin, now missing, passed to hold the bell firmly to its pole. The bell in Figure 143 supports the image of a bull which stands rigidly upon an oblong base. In the body of this bell are four apertures in the shape of triangles, the apexes of which are centered directly upon the sides of the base above. In all other respects, these bells differ only slightly.

In Figures 144 and 145 two separate views are presented of another bronze bell from Nagytarcsa, found at the same time that the ditchdiggers discovered the pole-top bells. The bell has a slit in its mantle similar to those in the Amlash bells shown in Figures 44 and 45. The clapper is missing. The bell dates from the late 6th to the 5th century B.C.

144

Since the latter part of the 19th century studies have been made and interesting conclusions have been drawn by archaeologists and researchers regarding the use to which pole-top bells were put by the Scythians. Less difficulty would have been experienced with certain finds were it not for the fact that many bells were discovered by workmen digging on civic projects or by clandestine diggers or by other individuals lacking archaeological knowledge. It is unfortunate that such people were, at times, either unable or unwilling to provide the information needed by scientists. A number of archaeologists have expressed opinions that pole-top bells were of ritualistic significance—that some were set up on poles as ritual objects within sanctuaries and that others were used in connection with religious, often magic, rites. Such rites were performed by a shaman, a priest whose position corresponded to that of a medicine man of a North or South American Indian tribe.

145

One of the many theories advanced by archaeologists is that Scythian pole-top bells crowned tents; another, that they served as ornaments on wagons; still another, that poles surmounted by bells were at times implanted in the ground to identify the tents of military leaders and titled personages. Another theory is that poles topped by bells were utilized to support the canopies of chieftains' chariots and of hearses. Several authorities have

Figure 146. Bronze bell (B 57–44). Ust-Kamenka, Dnepropetrovskii District, Ukrainian S.S.R. Late Sarmatian Period, 1st–2nd century A.D. Height 3.4 cm. (1 5/16 in.), diameter 2.5 cm. (1 in.). Patina brown. Courtesy of The State Historical Museum of the Ukrainian S.S.R., Kiev.

expressed the belief that the bells were placed on the ends of chariot draw poles to ward off evil spirits from the horses. Others have suggested that banners or streamers were hung below some of the pole-top bells, since a number of them are cast with small rings. Another opinion is that poles, crowned with bells, were borne as standards into battle ahead of the combatants; the figures of various animals on the bells may have identified the military units. All these various suppositions regarding the use of pole-top bells well merit consideration, for their uses may have been many indeed.

146

The Sarmatians The 5th century B.C. Greek historian and traveler Herodotus made the first recorded mention of the Sarmatians. He reported: "When one crosses the Tanais [now the Don], one is no longer in Scythia; the first region on crossing is that of the Sauromatae." Herodotus believed that they were descended from Amazonian women and Scythian youths. A people of Indo-European stock, whose ancestry and mores were long overlooked, the Sarmatians during the past thirty-odd years have been the subject of study by anthropologists, archaeologists, and prehistorians. Within that time we have learned much about these marauding tribesmen, whose history spanned a period of over one thousand years, from the 6th century B.C. to the 5th century A.D., and whose migrations covered a vast territory of more than 2,500 miles, from the Altai Mountains on the east to the waters of the Danube on the west.

The Sarmatians consisted of several tribes, differing in certain ways from one another. Like the Scythians, they were nomadic, even while following pastoral pursuits such as stockbreeding; they spent much time in the saddle. Mounted on fast steeds, they constantly fought neighboring tribesmen with sword, bow and arrow, lance and spear. They traveled about in wagons, stopping to pitch their tents of felt wherever good grazing lands were to be found. In some areas they occasionally engaged in agriculture and randomly hunted game. They left no written word.

By the 3rd century B.C. the power of the Scythians on the steppes of southern Russia had come to an end and was supplanted by the advancing Sarmatians and their tribes—the Roxolani, Iazyges, Alani, and others. In time, they too were forced from the

Figure 147. Bronze bell. Saudi Arabia. Circa 2nd century A.D. Length 9.2 cm. (3⅝ in.), width 5.4 cm. (2⅛ in.), depth 3.2 cm. (1¼ in.). Patina light green.

scene, and when the Alani finally were defeated by the Visigoths in Spain, much of Europe was under the domination of the Goths and the Huns.

The bell in Figure 146 was found in 1951 in barrow No. 5 of a Sarmatian burial ground near the village of Ust-Kamenka in the Dnepropetrovskii District, Ukrainian S.S.R. The burial ground dates from the 1st to the 2nd century A.D., and therefore belongs to the Late Sarmatian Period. Excavations were conducted at this Bronze Age site by the Nikopolskaia Archaeological Expedition, organized by the Archaeological Institute of the Academy of Sciences of the Ukrainian S.S.R. under the direction of E. V. Makhno. The bell is cone-shaped. Its body is pierced by six equally spaced triangular apertures; their apexes point alternately upward and downward. Groups of incised lines run diagonally across the sections between the apertures. Two lines encircle the bell's crown, while a third appears near the top of the bell's suspension ring. The clapper is missing.

The Arabian Peninsula

The comparatively few antiquities which have been discovered on the Arabian Peninsula have fired the imagination of the outside world, and it is widely believed that much archaeological treasure lies buried in the soil of such ancient kingdoms in the south as Ma'in, Saba (Sheba), Qataban, Hadhramaut, and Himyar and the northern site of Teyma (Taima or Tema of the Bible). Taima was the Arabian seat of the last priest-king of Babylon, Nabonidus (reigned 556–539 B.C.).

The bronze bell in Figure 147 reportedly came from a dig in a Saudi Arabian village on the Gulf of Aqaba at the northeastern extremity of the Red Sea. The bell is typical of many worn by domestic animals in that region and may be dated from about the 2nd century A.D. Its mouth has a distinct outward flare. The thin arched suspension section is part of the bell itself and is pierced by what was once a round hole, now deeply worn. Within the body of the bell a very corroded semicircular ring and a small piece of wire to hold the clapper are still present. The clapper is missing.

The bronze bell in Figure 148 came from a site on the edge of Khôr Rûri (ancient Sumhuram), a town located on an inlet of the Arabian Sea in the province of Dhofar, Sultanate of Oman.

147

The bell, which dates from about the 3rd to the 5th century A.D., was discovered in the early part of 1960 by an expedition of the American Foundation for the Study of Man, excavating under the direction of the archaeologist Ray L. Cleveland. Later a full report of the find was published in Bulletin No. 159 (October 1960) of the American Schools of Oriental Research. The bell, which is unique, was unearthed less than a meter below the surface. There is a circular opening in its dome below which originally hung a clapper. The clapper, now missing, was probably held in place after the prongs of its split upper end had been passed through the hole and bent in opposite directions. The bell's mouth is framed by a ring of round section. Just above it, barely visible through heavy incrustation, are three raised letters reading *syn*—i.e., *sin*, the name of the moon god, patron deity of Sumhuram.

The Near East

Figure 149. Bronze bell. Anatolia. Circa 400 B.C. Length 4.8 cm. (1⅞ in.). Patina dark green.

Figure 151. Bronze bell. Anatolia. Islamic Period, circa 10th–13th century A.D. Height 8.3 cm. (3¼ in.), diameter 9.2 cm. (3⅝ in.). Patina green.

149

151

Anatolia

On a map of the ancient Near East, Anatolia covers almost all of the western half of present-day Turkey. In the south lies Lycia; directly to the east, Keban. Beyond there, Urartu comprises the area in the neighborhood of Lake Van. The earliest mention of Anatolia occurs in a work known as the *King of Battle Epic*, which tells of contact between Purushkhanda, Anatolia's most important city, and Assyria. A legendary account is given therein of military forces being led to Purushkhanda by the Assyrian king, Sargon of Agade. However, it was not until the time of Erishum I of Assyria (reigned circa 1941–1902 B.C.) that the existence of an ancient relationship between Anatolia and Assyria was actually documented by discoveries of inscriptions unearthed at Kültepe in eastern Anatolia.

The bronze bell illustrated in Figure 149 reportedly was found in Anatolia. It is of pomegranate shape with four broad ribs, one of which apparently lost its form in the casting process. Above the ribs appear the heads of two dogs facing in opposite directions. Between them is a small hole permitting the bell to be worn as an amulet. The stylized calyx is quite large, considerably out of proportion to the body of the bell. No pellet is present.

Another bronze bell from Anatolia is shown in Figure 150. It is cast in the form of an ibex standing stock-still but with an alert expression, as if the animal were about to take flight. The bell has ten apertures: three appear between incised lines on each side of the animal's body; one on each side of its neck; and single ones on the back and belly. Diagonal and horizontal lines decorate its forequarters. The hooves have been cast with a slightly convex bar between them, which served as a hand grip when the bell was rung in religious ceremonies. A single pellet is present.

The bronze bell in Figure 151 was purchased in Istanbul. It is of the Islamic Period and dates from about the 10th to the 13th century A.D. Its clapper is missing. The suspension ring, which was cast with the bell, shows considerable wear. Four raised vertical motifs, rounded at the top, pointed at the bottom, and equidistant from one another, decorate its smooth outer surface. These motifs are similar to, though much wider than, those of the Sassanian bell of the 6th to the 7th century A.D. from Gurgan pictured in Figure 39. Both bells were probably worn by domestic animals.

Figure 150. Bronze religious ceremonial bell. Anatolia. Anatolian New Kingdom, 1475–1192 B.C. Height 11.3 cm. (4⁷⁄₁₆ in.), length 8.1 cm. (3³⁄₁₆ in.). Patina dark green. Courtesy of the Joseph Ternbach Collection.

Figures 152 and 153. Bronze bell.
Masada, Israel. 6th century B.C. Height
6.3 cm. (2½ in.), diameter 3.8 cm.
(1½ in.). Patina light brown. Courtesy
of Professor Y. Yadin and the Masada
Archaeological Expedition.

Israel

Many names have been given to that narrow strip of territory whose extensive coastline is washed by the waters of the eastern Mediterranean and which, before it became the state of Israel in 1948, was long known as Palestine. The land has been inhabited and governed by many peoples: Canaanites, Israelites, Hyksos, Hittites, Egyptians, Persians, Greeks, Romans, Turks, and others. All of them left evidence of their cultures amid its imposing monuments and within the stratified soil of its countless scattered mounds. Though much archaeological work has been carried out, comparatively few bells have been unearthed. The biblical reference to gold bells on the robe (ephod) of the high priest in the Book of Exodus, 28:33–35 and 39:25–26, should fire the imagination of those interested in bells and cause them to hope that someday an archaeologist will discover a hidden cache of golden bells beneath Jerusalem's ancient foundations.

One of the most rewarding archaeological projects in Israel was initiated at Masada, which until its fall in 73 A.D. stood as the last bastion of Jewish resistance in the Roman-Jewish War. From the ruins of that ancient majestic rock fortress in Israel has come a small bronze bell, depicted in Figures 152 and 153. The bell is of special interest because it probably was used continually for centuries before its ultimate burial amid rubble following the siege and capture of Masada by the Tenth Legion under the Roman governor Silva. The bell was discovered, together with many other objects, while excavations were being carried out between 1963 and 1965 by the Masada Archaeological Expedition under the direction of the distinguished archaeologist and author Yigael Yadin. The bell had, undoubtedly, hung from the neck of a donkey, which before the siege had followed a narrow and difficult path up the rock's western side to reach the top. This bell, which has been cleaned of incrustation, presents a number of interesting features. Its original clapper was suspended from a horizontal bar riveted to the bell's body. The bar is missing. One of the holes which held it remains open; the other is closed, filled with corrosion. The bell's characteristics identify it as of Asiatic rather than European origin. It may have been cast in Judea or brought into that land from the East. The bell resembles the one from Persepolis depicted in Figure 36. Both bells are of similar shape. Each was cast with its suspension ring elevated to a

Figure 155. Bronze bell. Gezer, Israel. Circa 350–600 A.D. Height 4.3 cm. (1¹¹⁄₁₆ in.). Patina reddish brown. Courtesy of the Department of Antiquities and Museums, Israel.

155

noticeable degree above the crown and each originally held a round bar to support a clapper.

The bell in its present state shows that it was repaired sometime during the Roman occupation of Judea, which began with the capture of Jerusalem by Pompey the Great (106–48 B.C.) in 64 B.C. The lost bar which held the original clapper was replaced by a ring, still present, soldered inside the bell's crown. It is characteristic of many Roman bells that a ring for the suspension of the clapper was cast as part of the bell. That this bell was used over a very long period of time during the Roman occupation of Judea is evidenced by the condition of the lower part of the ring, as seen in Figure 153. It is almost completely worn through from the friction of a swinging clapper, now missing.

A representation of a bell of somewhat similar form appears in the mosaic in Figure 154. The bell is suspended from the collar of a saddled donkey in one of a group of early 6th century A.D. mosaic panels which form the floor of the synagogue at Beit Alfa, a site near Hefsi Bah in the eastern Valley of Jezreel. The panels were discovered by chance in 1928 during the digging of a water channel. The foundations of the synagogue were unearthed in 1929 by the archaeologists E. L. Sukenik and N. Avigad, who were conducting excavations for the Hebrew University, Jerusalem. The mosaic panel in which the bell appears presents the scene of Abraham offering his son Isaac as a sacrifice to God. It is the joint work of the Jewish mosaicists Marianos and his son Hanina, who placed their names in Greek upon the piece.

The bronze bell shown in Figure 155 was found at Gezer in an elaborate tomb, No. 147, which from all appearances must have been that of a distinguished family. There was evidence that the tomb originally had been covered by a monumental building but that this building had been demolished and its stones removed from the site. The discovery of the tomb was made in the course of two excavations: one in 1902–5, the other in 1907–09. The expeditions were projects of the Palestine Exploration Fund under the direction of the well-known archaeologist R. A. Stewart Macalister. The bell lay in the third and principal chamber among a number of objects of little intrinsic value which had failed to interest robbers when they broke into the tomb some three hundred years before. The approximate date of the robbery was

Figure 156. Bronze bell. Jerusalem, Israel. 4th century A.D. Height 2.4 cm. (15⁄16 in.), diameter 2.1 cm. (13⁄16 in.). Patina reddish brown. Courtesy of the Department of Antiquities and Museums, Israel.

Figure 157. Bronze bell. Jish, Israel. Late 5th century A.D. Height 4.4 cm. (1¾ in.), diameter 2.8 cm. (1⅛ in.). Patina light brown. Courtesy of the Department of Antiquities and Museums, Israel.

indicated by a German 16th century coin minted in Nuremberg, found with the discarded goods. Besides the bell, excavators found a glass bracelet, still intact, some fragments of other bracelets, a number of clay lamps, a spatula, a nail, and two metal rings that may have been used as key rings.

In the winter of 1935–36, while reconstructing the road which leads from Jerusalem's St. Stephen's Gate (Bab el Asbat) in the city's east wall to the Jericho Road, workmen discovered beneath the old roadbed the masonry of a Roman tomb of the late 4th century A.D. The tomb yielded a quantity of Roman clay lamps and small glass vases, together with the bronze bell pictured in Figure 156. The outer surface of the bell is deeply corroded, and small sections of the crown and the clapper are missing. A twisted wire forms the bell's suspension loop.

In 1937, workmen removing rock in order to construct a cistern near a flour mill on the property of Hanna esh Sholi, on the outskirts of the village of Jish (the ancient Gischala), broke through the roof of a chamber containing a number of rock tombs. While the digging of a trench to reach the door of the chamber was proceeding under the direction of the archaeologist N. Makhouly, a second tomb chamber, containing shaft graves (*kokim*), was discovered. In one of these, grave No. 17, eight bells of different shapes were found. They are of the Byzantine Period and date from the late 5th century A.D. One of these bells, shown in Figure 157, is of the swinging-clapper type but the clapper is missing. From a double circular platform, two pointed extensions at the top of the bell overlap to form an arch and serve as the bell's suspension ring. Four lines encircle the bell at its waist.

The bronze bell depicted in Figure 158 was also discovered while the second chamber was being cleared. It lay in grave No. 15. The bell is cup-shaped and once supported a clapper, now missing. A wire twisted into a double loop serves as a means of suspension. It belongs to the Byzantine Period and dates from the late 5th century A.D. The bell shows much corrosion and bears two conspicuous white stains.

In 1952, the University of Chicago Oriental Institute sent an expedition under the field direction of Pinhas Delougaz to Khirbat Al-Karak (Ruin of the Fortress), one of the largest and most

156

157

Figure 158. Bronze bell. Jish, Israel. Late 5th century A.D. *Height 3.8 cm. (1½ in.), diameter 3.2 cm. (1¼ in.). Patina reddish brown. Courtesy of the Department of Antiquities and Museums, Israel.*

Figure 159. Bronze bells. Khirbat Al-Karak, Israel. Circa 350–600 A.D. *Average height 2 cm. (¾ in.). Patina light green, incrusted with soil. Courtesy of the Department of Antiquities and Museums, Israel.*

159

Figures 160–162. Bronze bell. Sidon, Phoenicia. Punic Period, circa 4th–3rd century B.C. Height 2.7 cm. (1¹⁄₁₆ in.), diameter 2.2 cm. (⅞ in.). Patina dark brown.

important archaeological sites in Israel. Khirbat Al-Karak lies at the southwestern end of Lake Tiberias, better known as the Sea of Galilee. The work there involved the excavation of a Byzantine church and a group of eight nearby Byzantine graves. All the graves had been looted, but a few bronze objects were found in them. In grave No. 3, the eight bronze bells shown in Figure 159 were discovered, all heavily corroded. Seven are of the crotal type. Of these only the second from the right in the top row contains a pellet. The open-mouthed bell at the extreme right of the lower row is in a badly crushed condition, and its clapper is missing.

The Phoenicians

No one people appears to have contributed more to the migration of bells by sea than the Phoenicians. Semites who first came into prominence as early as the second millennium B.C., they developed as a political entity in the narrow strip of territory generally referred to as Phoenicia. The country stretched northward along the eastern shore of the Mediterranean Sea from the city of Tyre (Es Sur) in Lebanon to the island of Arwad (Aradus) in Syria. Between these boundaries arose the important cities of Byblos (Jubayl) and Sidon (Saida). The Phoenicians established a rich kingdom; they took advantage of their geographical location to become a great maritime and commercial power throughout the whole Mediterranean, Aegean, and Black Sea areas. They later extended their activities to waters far beyond, both eastward and westward, and the reputation of their navigators spread far and wide. Herodotus recorded that in the 7th century B.C. the Egyptian Pharaoh Necho "sent a number of ships manned by Phoenicians" to circumnavigate Africa. These vessels sailed from the east coast of Egypt down the Red Sea, rounded the Cape of Good Hope, and returned to the Mediterranean via the Strait of Gibraltar. Phoenician ships traded in all the principal Mediterranean ports; from Sais (Sa el Hager) in the Nile Delta and nearby Pelusium in the east to Massilia (Marseilles) and other ports in the west. Out of the home port, Byblos, the famed cedars of Lebanon were shipped to mighty neighboring kings, including King Solomon (10th century B.C.), for the building of palaces and temples.

The bell shown in Figures 160–162 reportedly comes from Sidon.

160-162

148

Figure 163. Bronze bells. Ibiza, Spain. Punic Period, 5th–4th century B.C. Left to right: Height 6.5 cm. (2⁹⁄₁₆ in.), diameter 3.6 cm. (1⁷⁄₁₆ in.); height 4.2 cm. (1⅝ in.), diameter 2.4 cm. (1³⁄₁₆ in.); height 3.6 cm. (1⁷⁄₁₆ in.), diameter 1.7 cm. (¹¹⁄₁₆ in.); height 4 cm. (1⁹⁄₁₆ in.), diameter 2 cm. (⁹⁄₁₆ in.): Patina light green. Courtesy of the Museo Arqueológico, Barcelona.

Figure 164. Bronze bells. Ibiza, Spain. Punic Period, 5th–4th century B.C. Left to right: height 4.5 cm. (1¾ in.), diameter 3 cm. (1³⁄₁₆ in.); height 2.8 cm. (1⅛ in.), diameter 1.6 cm. (⅝ in.); height 3.8 cm. (1½ in.), diameter 2.3 cm. (⅞ in.); height 4.5 cm. (1¾ in.), diameter 2.8 cm. (1⅛ in.). Patina light green. Courtesy of the Museo Arqueológico, Barcelona.

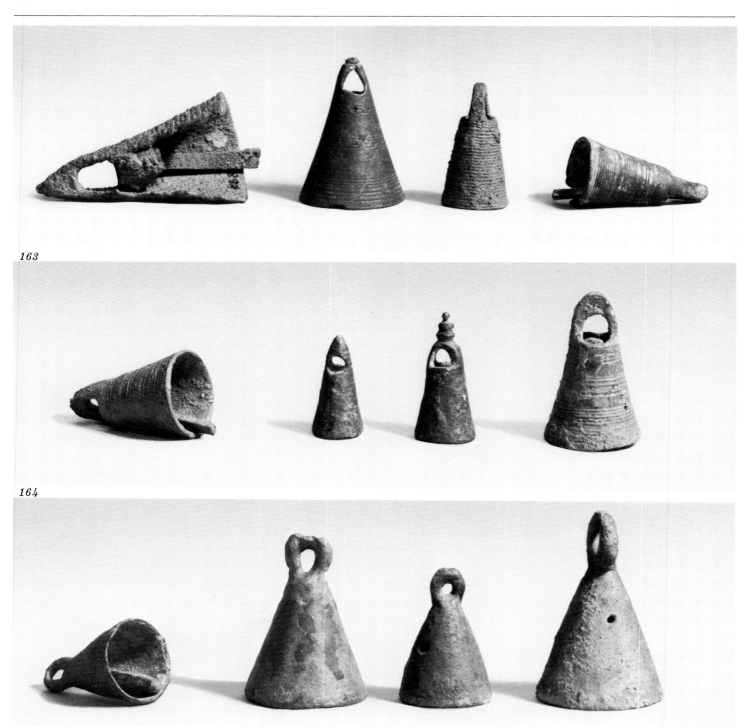

163

164

165

Figure 165. Bronze bells. Ibiza, Spain. Punic Period, 5th–4th century B.C. Left to right: height 4.3 cm. (1¹¹⁄₁₆ in.), diameter 2.7 cm. (1¹⁄₁₆ in.); height 5.3 cm. (2⅛ in.), diameter 3.6 cm. (1⁷⁄₁₆ in.); height 4.3 cm. (1¹¹⁄₁₆ in.), diameter 2.7 cm. (1¹⁄₁₆ in.); height 6 cm. (2⅜ in.), diameter 3.6 cm. (1⁷⁄₁₆ in.). Patina light green. Courtesy of the Museo Arqueológico, Barcelona.

Figures 166 and 167. Bronze bells. Ibiza, Spain. Punic Period, 5th–4th century B.C. 166: height 4 cm. (1⁹⁄₁₆ in.), diameter 3.7 cm. (1⁷⁄₁₆ in.). 167: height 4 cm. (1⁹⁄₁₆ in.), diameter 4 cm. (1⁹⁄₁₆ in.). Patina light green. Courtesy of the Museo Arqueológico, Barcelona.

It displays around its outside surface, equidistant in bold relief, the faces of three men, one bearded. It has a suspension ring and probably was worn as an article of personal adornment, having no religious significance.

Excavations at most of the sites where Phoenician colonies were established have yielded their share of bells. The first large Punic settlement outside Asia Minor was at Carthage (Tunis), believed to have been founded in 814 B.C. Other sites have been discovered on the islands of Cyprus, Rhodes, Crete, Corfu, Malta, Sicily, Sardinia, Corsica, Majorca, Minorca, and Ibiza; on the mainland of Spain, at Alicante and Gades (Cadiz); on the coast of Algeria, at Hippo (Bone); and at Leptis Magna on the coast of Tripolitania. Evidence of early Punic settlements in modern Morocco has been brought to light by excavations at Lalla Mimouna, Banasa, Sidi Slimane, and Mogador.

In 654 B.C. the Phoenicians established themselves in Spain and occupied it until about 150 B.C. A number of Punic bells were found on the island of Ibiza in 1910. The site was a necropolis just outside the town of Ibiza on the northern slope of a limestone hill called Puig dels Molins (Well of the Mill). It proved to be the largest Punic cemetery ever excavated, with some three thousand subterranean vaults. The work was carried out under the direction of the Spanish excavator A. Vives.

The bells shown in Figure 163 are conical in form. Concentric circles decorate their outer surfaces. The bell at the extreme left has a pointed crown. The second from the left terminates in a small button-like finial. The two sharp triangular openings on each side of the crown served for hanging the bell on a cord or chain. Punic bells, like most Assyrian bells, have swinging clappers which are suspended from horizontal bars riveted within their bodies and extend well below the bells' mouths. Examples are seen at the extreme left and right in Figure 163, as well as at the extreme left in Figure 164.

Figure 165 portrays four bells cast with round suspension rings.

The bodies of the bronze bells in Figures 166 and 167 are truncated. Suspension cords or wires once passed through the holes in their crowns. The holes in the waists of the bells indicate that they formerly held bars for clappers, now missing.

166-167

Europe

The Avars Many hypotheses by celebrated Chinese and European authorities have been advanced concerning the origin of the Avars. All point toward the conclusion that, like the Huns, they were of the Mongol race and originated in central Asia.

They were a nomadic people—primarily herdsmen. They developed no arts. However, seeking new grazing grounds and with a thirst for plunder, the Avars incessantly pushed westward, vanquishing the small tribes that stood in their path and absorbing them. Thus their numbers and their power constantly increased. Advancing north of the Caspian Sea, they settled for a time on the Kirgiz Steppes, generally termed the "Russian Steppes." In spite of the natural barrier of the Caucasus Mountains in the south, it was not long before they came into conflict with the Turks and for a while dominated them. Eventually the Turks rose in revolt and drove them back northward. At first they occupied the territory lying between the Volga and Danube rivers, just north of the Caucasus. They continued westward, crossing what is now the Ukrainian S.S.R. and passing north of the Carpathian Mountains. Finally, toward the second half of the 6th century A.D., they reached the plains of Hungary, where they established many settlements in the form of large fence-enclosed rings, the largest said to be thirty-eight miles (sixty-one kilometers) in circumference. Thousands of graves excavated at those sites have yielded their share of bells.

A series of new invasions, spearheaded by their cavalry, brought all of what is present-day Austria under Avar domination. In the area lying directly south of Vienna and stretching as far as Aspang are at least four excavated sites clearly established as of Avar occupation. Advancing westward, under their leader Bayan, they next invaded the lands of the Franks in 562 A.D. However, during the five-year period from 791 to 796 A.D., the Avars were practically annihilated by Charlemagne (742–814 A.D.) and were driven back east into Hungary. A small group of survivors settled there at a lake, the Plattensee, but less than a century later a plague wiped them out.

In both Austria and Hungary, Avar cemeteries have yielded bells of bronze and iron. The Avars used to bury a warrior and his horse either in the same grave or in separate graves one next to the

*Figures 168–172. Bronze bells. Vienna,
Austria. Avar, 7th–8th century A.D.
Height (average) 3.8 cm. (1½ in.).
Patina brown. Courtesy of the His-
torisches Museen der Stadt Wien.*

*Figures 173 and 174. Bronze bells.
Páhok, Zala County, Hungary. Avar,
8th century A.D. 173: height 3.5 cm.
(1⅜ in.). Patina light green. 174:
height 3.7 cm. (1⁷⁄₁₆ in.). Patina light
green. Courtesy of the Hungarian
National Museum, Budapest.*

168-172

173-174

Figures 175–180. Bronze and iron bells. Hungary. Avar, 8th century A.D. 175: Csáczár. Height 4.1 cm. (1⅝ in.), diameter 3.5 cm. (1⅜ in.). Patina dark green. 176: Cikó. Height 4.4 cm. (1¾ in.), width 4.2 cm. (1⅝ in.), depth 2.5 cm. (1 in.). Patina dark brown. 177: Pilismarót. Height 3.6 cm. (1⁷⁄₁₆ in.), diameter 3.8 cm. (1½ in.). Patina mottled, dark brown and dark green. 178: Pásztó. Height 6.2 cm. (2⁷⁄₁₆ in.), width 3.8 cm. (1½ in.). 179: Alattyán-Tulát. Height 3.2 cm. (1¼ in.), diameter 4.4 cm (1¾ in.). Patina mottled light green. 180: Szebény. Height 5.9 cm. (2⁵⁄₁₆ in.), diameter 2.5 cm. (1 in.). Patina dark brown, heavily rusted. Courtesy of the Hungarian National Museum, Budapest.

175-180

Figures 181 and 182. Bronze bell. Jánoshida, Hungary. Avar, 8th century A.D. Front and back views: height 2.6 cm. (1½₃₂ in.). Patina greenish brown. Courtesy of the Hungarian National Museum, Budapest.

other. It is interesting to note that in Hungary Avar bells have been discovered in the graves of warriors, but none has been found in those of horses. Moreover, most of the Avar bells unearthed there have come from the graves of infants and of boys from eight to ten years old and girls between the ages of fifteen and eighteen.

The five bronze crotal-type bells of which side and bottom views are shown in identically arranged rows in Figures 168–172 were excavated in 1943 from graves discovered on the slopes of Liesing, a suburb of Vienna. They are double-throated, with the exception of the one in Figure 171 which is trisected—an unusual form. Each bell holds a single pellet. The bell in Figure 170 bears apparently identical designs of two human faces, back to back. Holes portray the eyes, and the other features of the face are suggested by rope-shaped bands in high relief.

181

It is noteworthy that similar crotal-type bells, but with other designs on their surfaces, appeared later, not only elsewhere in Europe but also in the United States and Canada. Thirty or more such bells were often attached to a long leather strap to fit around a horse's belly. They are still to be found in certain rural areas and emit cheerful, tinkling sounds as horse-drawn sleighs glide over the snow.

In Figures 173 and 174 are two bronze bells of the 8th century A.D. which were discovered in separate graves in a cemetery at Pahok, Zala County, Hungary. The bell in Figure 174, excavated in 1885, is double-throated and contains one iron pellet. The one in Figure 173, found in 1881, is single-throated and holds a stone pellet.

182

Of much interest is a bronze effigy bell, shown in Figures 181 and 182, found at Janoshida, Hungary, in 1933. On one side appears the full face of a mustachioed and bearded man, while on the other side is the face of another with mustache only. The pellet is missing. This bell was worn as an object of adornment.

Figures 175–180 present bells of the 8th century A.D., also excavated from Hungarian cemeteries. The one in Figure 175 is bronze and was found at Császár in 1903. Inside its crown only fragments of its clapper remain. Figures 176 and 180 show bells unearthed at Cikó in 1894. They were excavated in a badly rusted condition, one telescoped within the other. The larger, lower one still holds a four-sided clapper, forced upward into the body of the bell. In

Figure 177 is a bronze bell, without clapper, discovered in 1941 in a woman's grave at Pilismarót, northwest of Budapest and not far from the Czechoslovakian border. The bell in Figure 178 was found in 1889 in a man's grave at Pásztó, Heves County, forty miles (sixty-four kilometers) northeast of Budapest. No clapper is present. In Figure 179 is a bronze bell, without clapper, found in 1934 at Alattyán-Tulát. In Figure 180 is an iron bell discovered in 1935 in a cemetery at Szebény. The bell is heavily damaged by corrosion, and its clapper is missing.

Greece Most bells which have been unearthed in Greece and on some of her island possessions were originally votive offerings in temples or gifts placed in human graves at the time of burial; and some were gifts to the living. Many of the latter had served as articles of personal adornment.

In 1914 some archaeologists directed their attention to Velestinon, a town in Thessaly which in ancient times was called Pherae. They suspected that a temple once stood about one quarter of a mile to the northwest of its ramparts, alongside the road to Larissa. Parts of broken stone columns had been noticed scattered about the area. In 1920 excavations confirmed the existence of such a temple, identified as dedicated to Zeus Thaulios. It dates from the end of the 4th century B.C., but its construction may have begun as early as the end of the 5th century B.C. The belief that a more ancient temple once occupied the same site was expressed by many, including the eminent Greek archaeologist A. Arvanitopolous.

As a result, the French School at Athens carried out further excavations and uncovered an ancient necropolis of the Geometric Period below the foundations of Zeus Thaulios. It yielded many skeletons but relatively few objects. However, in the surrounding grounds diggers in 1926 happened on a depository. It contained a large quantity of fibulae, finger rings, bracelets, pins, bronze figures of animals, including those of horses and birds, and a number of bells. All were votive offerings brought to the sanctuary.

It was long the custom among the Greeks, as among the Lurs, Scythians, and other nomadic Asiatic people, to put figures of birds atop some bells because of the belief that at death the

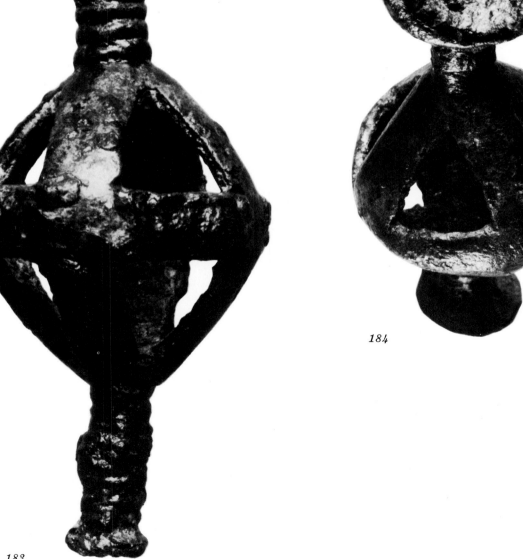

Figure 183. Bronze bell pendant. Pherae, Thessaly, Greece. Late Geometric Period, 8th century B.C. Height 8.2 cm. (3⅛ in.), diameter 2.3 cm. (⅞ in.). Patina dark green. Courtesy of the National Archaeological Museum, Athens.

Figure 184. Bronze bell. Pherae, Thessaly, Greece. Late Geometric Period, 8th century B.C. Height 1.5 cm. (19⁄32 in.), diameter 2.3 cm. (29⁄32 in.). Patina dark green. Courtesy of the National Archaeological Museum, Athens.

183

184

Figure 186. Bronze bell. Pherae, Thessaly, Greece. Archaic Period, 7th–6th century B.C. Height 3.5 cm. (1⅜ in.), diameter 3.5 cm. (1⅜ in.). Patina dark brown. Courtesy of the National Archaeological Museum, Athens.

Figure 185. Bronze bell. Pherae, Thessaly, Greece. Archaic Period, 7th–6th century B.C. Height 5.1 cm. (2 in.), diameter 2.8 cm. (1⅛ in.). Patina dark brown. Courtesy of the National Archaeological Museum, Athens.

186

soul assumed the form of a bird in flight. As for the bells found at Pherae, there may have been an added reason why the representations of birds were placed upon them: the prevalence of wild waterfowl at nearby Lake Boebeis.

The bronze bell pendant in Figure 183 was one of the objects excavated at the site of the Temple of Zeus Thaulios. It is of the Late Geometric Period and may be dated about the 8th century B.C. Its top, in the form of a duck with pronounced flat bill and square tail, rests upon a corrugated column above a crotal; a shorter column extends directly below. The body of the duck is pierced with a hole for suspension purposes. No pellet is present.

Identified as of the same era and provenance is the bronze bell portrayed in Figure 184. The bird which surmounts it has a very long bill and a swallow-like tail. The pellet is missing.

Influence from the Far East is evident in the design of a bell from Pherae, shown in Figure 185. It represents in stylized form a seven-sided pagoda with a window piercing each of the sides. It is of the Archaic Period and dates from about the 7th to the 6th century B.C. The swinging clapper, now missing, was originally suspended from a bronze bar which is still present in the bell's crown. It is interesting to see that this bell possesses several features like those of the Urartean bronze bells in Figures 120–122—namely, the circular suspension ring, the window-shaped apertures, and the bar for the suspension of a clapper.

The cone-shaped bell from Pherae shown in Figure 186 is also of the Archaic Period and was cast sometime between the 7th and 6th centuries B.C. It has a very dark brown patina. There are two holes in the crown of the bell from which a swinging clapper, now missing, originally hung.

From digs at Potidaea, Macedonia, comes the 8th century B.C. bronze bell pendant shown in Figure 187. It is crowned by the form of a bird which has been pierced for the insertion of a suspension cord. The entire piece is heavily corroded and no pellet is present.

In that category, a very interesting example is the bronze bell pendant from Macedonia portrayed in Figure 188. It is of the

185

Figure 187. Bronze bell. Potidaea, Macedonia, Greece. Late Geometric Period, 8th century B.C. *Height 8.3 cm. (3¼ in.). Patina light green with incrustation. Courtesy of the Trustees of The British Museum. London.*

Figure 188. Bronze bell pendant. Macedonia, Greece. Geometric Period, 9th–8th century B.C. *Height 9.5 cm. (3¾ in.). Patina dark green. Courtesy of The Metropolitan Museum of Art, New York, Edith Perry Chapman Fund, 1947.*

187-189

Figure 189. Bronze bell. Greece. Late Geometric Period, 8th–7th century B.C. Height 9.5 cm. (3¾ in.). Patina light green.

Figures 190 and 191. Terra-cotta bells. Boeotia, Greece. Second half of 5th century B.C. 190: height 8.3 cm. (3¼ in.), diameter 6.7 cm. (2⅝ in.). 191: height 6.3 cm. (2½ in.), diameter 6.1 cm. (2⅜ in.).

190

191

Geometric Period. On top is the form of a man, seated with his feet resting against the crotal-type bell below. Underneath the bell is an extension.

Figure 189 shows a Greek bronze object of the 8th to the 7th century B.C. Various opinions have been offered as to its use. One authority, U. Jantzen, writing in an article in the *Archaologischer Anzeiger, Beiblatt zum Jahrbuch des Deutschen Archaologischen Instituts* in 1953, put forth the suggestion that it may have been a bottle stopper, its knob wrapped with a resin-soaked cord. C. Rolley, in *Collection Helene Stathatos III, Objets Antiques et Byzantins* (Strasbourg, 1963), favors the theory that it was a pendant. The present writer concurs with the latter but believes that the object also served as a bell which rang when shaken and contained pellets the size of peppercorns. Those pellets rolled freely up and down within each of the four parallel vertical shafts formed by vertical rows of minute disks. The top and bottom edges of the disks are joined one above the other and resemble the heads of tiny mushrooms; their delicate stems issue horizontally from a thin bar running straight down the center of the bell. The top of the bell is surmounted by the figure of a squatting monkey. Its elbows rest on its knees, and its hands are brought together, touching its mouth in what might be regarded as a suppliant attitude. The back of the figure carries a crisscross design of delicately incised lines. The bell has a light green patina with some brown patches. The open space at the top just below the monkey's snout provides for the passing of a suspension cord. It has an extension below like the other bells worn as pendants portrayed in Figures 183, 184, 187, and 188. That feature, common to all of them, may indicate that the Greek artisans who cast the bells were influenced by the stylized calyxes on pomegranate-shaped bells brought from the East. The bell shown in Figure 189 is not unique; other bells of identical form have come from excavations in Potidaea.

Many terra-cotta bells, originally placed as votive offerings, have been unearthed in Boeotia, where the two shown in Figures 190 and 191 were reportedly found. They are decorated with painted brown markings and date from the second half of the 5th century B.C. There is a large hole at the top of the crown of each bell. The clappers are missing. (A lead seal was wired to each of these bells

192-194

Figures 192–194. Pottery bell. Greece. 2nd–3rd century A.D. Height 7.5 cm. (2¹⁵⁄₁₆ in.), diameter 4.5 cm. (1¹²⁄₁₆ in.). Patina grayish white. Courtesy of the Bibliothèque Nationale, Paris.

Figure 195. Bronze bell. Thebes, Greece. 4th century B.C. Height 6.4 cm. (2½ in.), diameter 4.2 cm. (1⅝ in.). Patina light brown. Courtesy of the Trustees of The British Museum, London.

in 1967 by the Bureau of Antiquities in Athens to indicate permission to take the bells out of Greece.)

The 4th century B.C. bronze bell in Figure 195 was discovered shortly before 1893 in excavations at the Temple of the Cabiri at Thebes (Thebae). On its surface three lines of punctured Greek characters declare its donor to be "Pyrrhias." The patina is a mottled light brown and light green. There is a very small hole at the top of its crown for the suspension of a clapper, now missing. The Cabiri were a group of two males and two females that were venerated as deities of fertility. They were also worshipped for their power to bring protection from all perils, especially from the sea. Though probably of Phrygian origin, they were frequently called the Samothracian Gods since they were identified with mysteries celebrated on the island of Samothrace. Devotion was shown to them throughout northern and central Greece and particularly in Macedonia and Boeotia, while their cult continued to flourish in Phrygia and other parts of Asia Minor.

The clay bell in Figures 192–194 dates from the 2nd to the 3rd century A.D. Details of its provenance are unknown. It appears to have been a personal gift bestowed upon an individual about to leave on a trip. Cast in high relief is a legend in Greek which runs completely around the sound bow of the bell. The part reading "Good Voyage" is shown in Figure 192, while that reading "Good Luck" is portrayed in Figure 194. The bell's clay clapper, partially visible in Figure 193, has been rehung on a string.

195

Yugoslavia

Although the early inhabitants of present-day Yugoslavia apparently had a knowledge of metallurgy as early as the third millennium B.C., they made little effort to put it to general use until the first half of the second millennium B.C. This was in marked contrast to the use of bronze by craftsmen of the Far East, Asia Minor, and some islands of the Aegean and Mediterranean, who quickly applied themselves to the fashioning of bronze weapons, bells, and other functional articles as soon as the knowledge of the technique became available to them. From the beginning of its Bronze Age, Yugoslavia was a land whose people engaged primarily in farming and pastoral pursuits. Settled in small communities, they traveled about in four-wheeled carts

Figure 196. Bronze breast ornament with bells. Vinica, Yugoslavia. Early "Hallstatt" Iron Age, 6th century B.C. Height 8.3 cm. (3¼ in.), width 11 cm. (4⁵⁄₁₆ in.). Patina light grayish green. Courtesy of the Peabody Museum, Harvard University.

drawn by horses. In less peaceful times these same animals bore their riders in combat and on predatory raids.

The bronze breast ornament portrayed in Figure 196 originally held a group of sixteen spherical bells, of which only eight remain, all without pellets. It was found in an Early "Hallstatt" Iron Age grave, No. 275, of the cemetery at Vinica, a small town in the western part of the country. Vinica had been established in the 6th century B.C. by the Japodes, an Illyrian-speaking tribe called Ipayges by the Romans. The tribe had migrated from Italy, making its way through mountain and river basins and finally settling in the Kupa River valley. It also established settlements at Prozor and Kompolje.

From 1905 until the outbreak of World War I in 1914, numerous archaeological expeditions were conducted to the Vinica necropolis. Excavations carried out by one of them, directed by the Grand Duchess of Mecklenburg-Schwerin, Germany, led to the discovery of the aforementioned breast ornament. The Grand Duchess was the wife of Grand Duke Paul Friedrich; undoubtedly because of her marriage to one of the few ruling princes of Slavonic origin in Germany, she had become interested in digging in that corner of the Austro-Hungarian Empire which after the war became part of Yugoslavia. In support of her project the Grand Duchess received encouragement, as well as financial assistance, from both Kaiser Wilhelm II of Germany and Emperor Franz Josef of Austria.

The Villanovans

Of unusual interest are the flat bronze bells excavated with the cinerary jars of the Villanovans. The Villanovans, named for a village on the banks of the Idice, a stream about five miles (eight kilometers) east of Bologna, Italy, flourished from the 9th to the 6th century, and perhaps even until the 5th century B.C. From almost the beginning of the Iron Age the Villanovans lived in close proximity to the Etruscans; gradually, they succumbed to the strong influence of expanding Etruscan culture and ultimately lost their independent identity.

The discovery in 1853 of an ancient necropolis in Villanova marked the first of a long series of important excavations throughout the Bologna area. Several of these Villanovan cemeteries, which yielded bells of the gong variety, lay outside

197

Porta Sant'Isaia and Porta Castiglione. A considerable number of these cemeteries were named after landowners upon whose properties they were discovered, as, for example, the Benacci cemetery, where the four bells illustrated in Figures 197, 198, 199, and 200 were found. These bells fall within the Second Benacci Period (950–750 or 700 B.C.).

The bells illustrated in Figures 201 and 202 were excavated at the Arsenale cemetery, so named since it is located at the site of an Italian arsenal. They belong to the Arnoaldi Period (750 or 700–500 B.C.). Meandrous-shaped symbols of unexplained significance appear, more or less distinctly, on all six bells. In some cases, the bell is a solid plate, as that shown in Figure 198; in others, as in Figures 197, 199, 200, 201, and 202, the bells contain either a single aperture or a geometrical arrangement of apertures. Inlays of amber decorate the bells portrayed in Figures 197 and 202. Amber was prized by the Villanovans, as it has been by most peoples as far back as the Stone Age. Though much amber was brought down from the Baltic by traders, there is scientific evidence that the Villanovans, particularly those at Bologna and Marzabotto, obtained it from the province of Emilia (now Emilia Romagna) or from Sicily.

Each bell was cast with an opening in the handle which permitted it to be hung on a wall or door, or held in one hand and struck with a baton held in the other. An examination of the bronze batons (Figures 198, 199, and 200) discloses that they are hollow from end to end. Consequently, it may be surmised that, for convenience, one end of a long cord was attached to the handle of the bell, while the other was passed through the baton and held in place by a large knot. These bells may have served a practical purpose in the homes of the Villanovans. Whether their presence in graves, along with other personal possessions, had any religious association with a belief in a future life is an unanswered question.

Each bell looks like the head of a battle-ax of yore. The bell's shape possibly had a symbolic significance as an instrument of sacrifice or a traditional meaning as a common weapon signifying military prowess. A further possibility is that the bell was given the shape of a battle-ax because in ancient times an ax head, resounding to a sharp blow, may have served as a bell.

Figure 197. Bronze bell. Villanova, Italy. Villanovan, Second Benacci Period, 950–750 or 700 B.C. Length 9.8 cm. (3⅞ in.), width 7.2 cm. (2¹³⁄₁₆ in.). Patina dark green. Courtesy of the Museo Civico Archeologico, Bologna.

Figure 198. Bronze bell and bronze baton. Villanova, Italy. Villanovan, Second Benacci Period, 950–750 or 700 B.C. Length 13.2 cm. (5³⁄₁₆ in.), width 10.8 cm. (4¼ in.). Patina light green. Length of baton 11.5 cm. (4½ in.). Courtesy of the Museo Civico Archeologico, Bologna.

198

Figure 199. Bronze bell and bronze
baton. Villanova, Italy. Villanovan,
Second Benacci Period, 950–750 or 700
B.C. Length 13.3 cm. (5¼ in.), width
11.3 cm. (4⁷⁄₁₆ in.). Patina yellowish
green. Length of baton 14.6 cm. (5¾
in.). Courtesy of the Museo Civico
Archeologico, Bologna.

Figure 200. Bronze bell and bronze baton. Villanova, Italy. Villanovan, Second Benacci Period, 950–750 or 700 B.C. Length 12.4 cm. (4⅞ in.), width 9.9 cm. (3⅞ in.). Patina dark green. Length of baton 11.4 cm. (4½ in.). Courtesy of the Museo Civico Archeologico, Bologna.

200

Figure 201. Bronze bell. Villanova, Italy. Villanovan, Arnoaldi Period, 750 or 700–500 B.C. Length 16.6 cm. (6½ in.), width 14.2 cm. (5⅝ in.). Patina light green. Courtesy of the Museo Civico Archeologico, Bologna.

Figure 202. Bronze bell. Villanova, Italy. Villanovan, Arnoaldi Period, 750 or 700–500 B.C. Length 16.5 cm. (6½ in.), width 16.7 cm. (6⁹⁄₁₆ in.). Patina dark green. Courtesy of the Museo Civico Archeologico, Bologna.

202

Figure 203. Bronze bell. Bisenzio, Italy. Etruscan, 6th century B.C. Height 4 cm. (1⁹⁄₁₆ in.), diameter 3.2 cm. (1¼ in.). Patina light green. Courtesy of the Museo Nazionale di Villa Giulia, Rome.

203

The Etruscans The Etruscan Period, which followed the Villanovan Period, extended from the end of the 6th century to the beginning of the 4th century B.C. The Etruscans were a mercantile maritime people who traded, as did the Phoenicians, throughout the entire Mediterranean area and brought home many articles of artistic merit. They moored their ships in ports of the Tyrrhenian Sea, such as Pyrgi, ten miles (sixteen kilometers) from the ancient town of Caere (Cerveteri), and Graviscae, a short distance from Tarquinia. Thriving Etruscan towns to the east, Marzabotto for example, utilized the harbors of Atria and Spina (near modern Comacchio) on the Adriatic. The Etruscans worshipped several Greek deities as well as their own; some counterparts of their own deities were found in the Greek pantheon.

Evidence of the existence of Etruscan bells is based upon a single bronze bell now in the Museo Nazionale di Villa Giulia in Rome. That bell, shown in Figure 203, was discovered in a tomb chamber (No. 2) of the 6th century B.C. in the necropolis of ancient Bisentium (Bisenzio). This site lies near the modern town of Capodimonte in Latium, near Viterbo. Unlike the tomb chambers of Tarquinia, all those of ancient Bisentium were unpainted. Tomb chambers were regarded as homes for the dead and were made to appear as such, with the bodies in them laid upon stone couches.

The bell from Bisentium may have belonged to the deceased person in life or may have been placed in the tomb at the time of burial as a gift. Perhaps other bells may be found in the approximately 25,000 Etruscan tombs yet to be excavated. The hundreds of tombs at Tarquinia, richest of all those excavated so far, and the tomb chambers under the tumuli at nearby Cerveteri have so far yielded no bells. Nor do the exquisitely painted murals in Tarquinia's underground burial chambers depict bells upon horses or other animals. At Marzabotto, near Bologna, where important excavations have been made, no Etruscan bells have ever been found, nor have military burials with horses or weapons ever been uncovered there.

The Bisentium bell is dome-shaped. A section at the bottom has broken off and has been lost. Apparently the bell was affected by humidity and disintegrated as it lay on its side in the tomb. On the bell's light green patina faint traces of silver are still

visible in a small section above the break, indicating that a silver wash originally covered its outer surface. A wire handle, the extension of which once supported a clapper, now missing, is fastened into a small opening in the crown.

Ireland

Judging from the hoards uncovered in Ireland dating from around 800 B.C., bronze objects began to appear in some abundance in Ireland at that time. Among the goods unearthed were many weapons, such as spearheads and swords, but objects of a utilitarian, domestic character also were discovered. These included cauldrons, buckets, knives, hammers, axes, and numerous bells. One of the most important archaeological treasures is the famous Dowris Hoard, discovered in 1825 at Dowris, County Offaly. This find yielded at least forty-eight bells of the crotal type, which can be regarded as belonging to the transition period between the Late Bronze Age and the Early Iron Age of Ireland (circa 700–500 B.C.).

Although the shape of the spherical bells in the hoard was probably inspired by bells introduced into Ireland from the Continent, the features of the pear-shaped bells are probably uniquely Irish. The use of both types is obscure.

A careful examination of the bells in Figures 204–210 reveals that each bell was made of separately cast halves sealed together vertically after the insertion of a pellet. An unusual feature is that each was made without mouth, slit, or other aperture, so that when shaken they give forth a dull rattling sound.

Several of the pear-shaped bells have holes—evidence of their having been broken into by treasure seekers; fissures appear in each of the spherical ones. In relief around the upper third part of each of the five pear-shaped bells runs a series of ribs—in three cases, twelve in number, and in two cases, fourteen—adding a decorative touch to otherwise plain surfaces. Each of the bells is made with a small suspension ring through which a larger ring has been passed.

174

204-207

208-210

The Romans and Iberians in Spain

About 180 miles (290 kilometers) up the Guadiana River is the modern city of Badajoz, Spain. It was founded in 25 B.C. as the Roman town of Augusta Emerita (Merida) under the leadership of Agrippa, lieutenant of Emperor Augustus, and served as headquarters for a Roman legion and a place of retirement for veterans who had completed their service. Augusta Emerita became the capital of the Roman province of Lusitania. Extensive archaeological excavations, which were started there in 1910 by Jose Ramon Melida and which continued over the years, have brought forth what are generally regarded as Spain's largest and most important and impressive Roman ruins. However, even prior to 1910, numerous archaeological discoveries were sporadically made there. Among the finds was a small and unusually interesting object which has been given the name "The Wagon of Merida" (Figures 211 and 212). It is believed to have been discovered at Merida about the latter quarter of the 19th century. Soon thereafter, it became part of a private collection in Badajoz. The archaeologist Robert Forrer purchased the little bronze wagon in 1930 and presented it to the Musée des Antiquités Nationales in the Château at Saint-Germain-en-Laye (Seine et Oise), France. Professor Forrer has identified it as an Iberian work. This would probably place the date of the wagon's origin prior to the 6th century B.C., when the largest Celtic migration into Spain from the lands north of the Pyrenees took place. A fusion of Celtic and Iberian cultures gradually produced a new culture—the Celtiberian.

It is interesting to observe the strong resemblance which the bells of the Iberian wagon bear to the Nimrud bells, not only because of the close similarity of their suspension arches, but also because the clappers in both hang from bars riveted within their bodies. On the supposition that Iberian craftsmen in this instance were influenced by the art of a foreign culture, such as the Assyrian, little imagination is required to picture Phoenician ships from the nearby Punic settlement of Gades (Cadiz) making their way up the Guadiana River to Mérida, their holds filled with much-sought merchandise from Asia Minor—including bronze bells of the Nimrud type.

The platform of this miniature wagon supports the figure of a hunter, spear in hand, astride a horse. At his left, a barking dog

Figures 211 and 212. Bronze wagon with bronze bells. Mérida, Spain. Iberian Period, 6th–5th century B.C. Wagon length 28 cm. (11 1/32 in.), width 10.5 cm. (4 1/8 in.). Patina dark brown. Bells: average height 1.9 cm. (3/4 in.), average diameter 1 cm. (3/8 in.). Patina dark brown. Courtesy of the Musée des Antiquités Nationales, Château de Saint-Germain-en-Laye (Yvelines), France.

211

accompanies him as he rides in hot pursuit of a wild boar. Holes in the platform of the wagon indicate that originally the figure of another dog stood at the right. The group is closely identified with the life of an age when the sport of hunting wild boars was popular not only in Spain but throughout most of Europe.

Cast in one piece with the horse is a small ring directly below its lower jaw; from the ring hangs a three-link chain holding a single bronze bell. Five similar bells are suspended in a row on chains from the rear of the wagon. However, only two of the bells appear to be the original ones. The wagon was probably a child's toy. In its day, it apparently received rather rough treatment, for there is a break at the front of the platform in the center. A ring probably was attached at this point to enable the child to drag the wagon along at the end of a cord. According to ancient custom, the toy may have been placed in the child's grave, either as an accompaniment to afterlife or as a votive offering.

The bronze bell shown in Figure 213 was excavated on the island of Mallorca. Except for a series of incised lines running around its body, it has the distinct features of the Iberian bells portrayed in Figures 211 and 212. Like them, it resembles those from Nimrud in Figures 96–101. Noteworthy are two small holes in the body of the bell into which a bar supporting a clapper was formerly riveted. Both bar and clapper are now missing. The bell is attached to carefully twisted copper wires, which form a band for a child's wrist. The practice of placing a bracelet with a bell around a child's wrist was common in most Mediterranean lands for centuries, not only to ward off evil spirits but also, by its tinkle, to disclose the whereabouts of the little wanderer.

Native resistance to Roman occupation of the Iberian Peninsula lasted for more than two centuries. In their final struggle for independence, the Celtiberians were led in guerrilla warfare by the heroic Lusitanian shepherd Viriathus. In 139 B.C., a combination of Roman bribery and treachery effected his assassination; consequently, resistance to Roman domination subsided, and in 133 B.C., under the command of Scipio the Younger, Rome achieved a total victory with the siege and fall of the Celtiberian town of Numantia.

Dating to about the 1st century A.D. and excavated in Spain is

212

213

214

the Roman bronze bell shown in Figure 214. The bell was cast with a circular opening in its top. A bar within the crown supports a swinging clapper.

The Romans at Pompeii Although Pompeii is known to have existed even before the 6th century B.C., it was not until 80 B.C. that it became a Roman colony known as Colonia Cornelia Veneria Pompeiorum. As such, it continued until August 24, 79 A.D., when it was suddenly buried under a rain of hot ashes and cinders and completely destroyed by the volcanic eruption of nearby Mount Vesuvius.
Periodic excavations at the site of this buried city have been made as far back as 1748. As a result, a considerable number of bells have been brought to light from time to time. These bells are typical in form of many unearthed at other Roman sites. Many bells found at Pompeii measure only a few inches in height (Figures 216–218). They either served as votive offerings or were worn as talismans; some were suspended from the necks of household pets. Larger bells, such as the one shown in Figure 215, were often hung from the necks of cattle. The ashes which fell upon Pompeii and covered up this bell scorched and deeply scarred its surface. In sharp contrast, a quite similar bell (Figure 221) found at Herculaneum fared much better. Of about the same size were the bells hung around the ankles of war captives brought to Rome to be marched in chains behind the chariots of their conquerors.
Aside from the general belief throughout the ancient world that bells possessed a particular power to ward off evil spirits, the hanging of bells on the necks of domestic animals served the practical purpose of frightening off roving wild beasts, which attacked especially at night.
Of particular interest are the bronze lamps which were hung at the entrances of shops and private dwellings. Those outside of homes were placed at the right of doorways under the peristyles facing the inner courtyards. The bells which were suspended on chains from these lamps were believed to give protection by day against the dreaded power of the sun and by night against all evil influences. Lamps were also found in each bedchamber (*cubiculum*). Figure 219 shows a bronze lamp with six bells. Two of these bells, and the lamp itself, hang from the genitals of a

Figure 215. Bronze bell. Pompeii, Italy. Roman Period, 1st century A.D. *Height 14 cm. (5½ in.), width 9.8 cm. (3⅞ in.), depth 7.9 cm. (3⅛ in.). Patina light green, deeply scorched and incrusted with ashes. Courtesy of the Museo Nazionale, Naples.*

Figures 216–218. Bronze bells. Pompeii, Italy. Roman Period, 1st century A.D. *216: height 5.4 cm. (2⅛ in.), diameter 4.5 cm. (1¾ in.). 217: height 7.9 cm. (3⅛ in.), diameter 5.7 cm. (2¼ in.). 218: height 5.3 cm. (2¹⁄₁₆ in.), diameter 4.2 cm. (1⅝ in.). Patina mottled green, light and dark green. Courtesy of the Museo Nazionale, Naples.*

215

216-218

Figure 219. Bronze lamp with bells.
Pompeii, Italy. Roman Period, 1st cen-
tury A.D. *Lamp: height, overall 46.3 cm.*
(18¼ in.). Bells: average height 4.5
cm. (1¾ in.), average diameter 3.2 cm.
(1¼ in.). Patina light green, incrusted
with ashes. Courtesy of the Museo
Nazionale, Pompeii.

Figure 220. Bronze lamp with bells.
Pompeii, Italy. Roman Period, 1st cen-
tury A.D. *Lamp: height, overall 51.7 cm.*
(20⅜ in.). Bells: average height 3.8 cm.
(1½ in.), average diameter 3.2 cm.
(1¼ in.). Patina light green, incrusted
with ashes. Courtesy of the Museo
Nazionale, Pompeii.

219-220

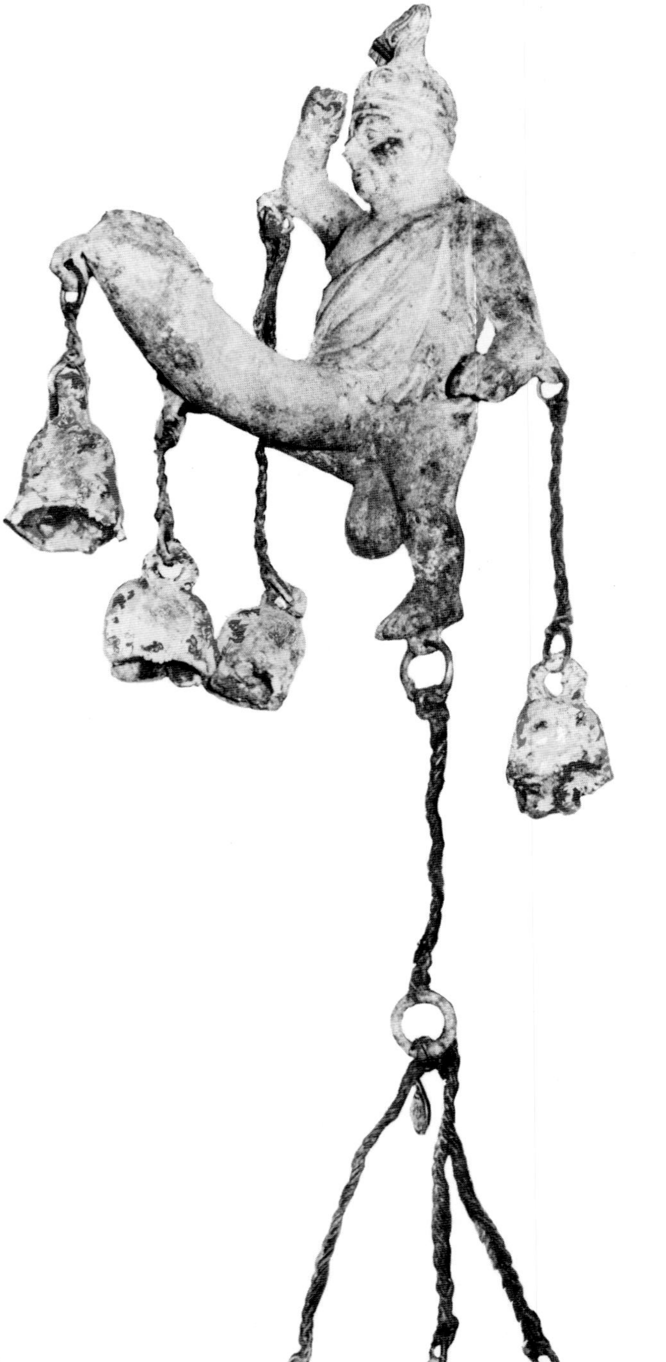

Figure 221. Bronze bell. Herculaneum, Italy. Roman Period, 1st century A.D. Height 17.2 cm. (6¾ in.), width 10.1 cm. (4 in.), depth 7.6 cm. (3 in.). Patina green with blue cast. Courtesy of the Museo Nazionale, Naples.

bronze figure of the god of male procreative power, Priapus. Accentuating the lascivious character of Priapus, smaller genitals have been superimposed upon his phallus. The god holds a bell in his left hand, while in his right he clasps a small inverted rhyton (drinking horn). Of the six bells only the bottom one has retained its clapper. It is very much corroded.

Figure 220 shows a bronze lamp with four bells. The actual oil receptacle is suspended from the left foot of an image of a dwarf. A bell hangs from his right foot, while another hangs from each arm; the right arm is raised in a triumphant gesture. A fourth bell hangs from the extremity of his exaggerated phallus. Within all the bells are fragments of heavily corroded clappers.

A short distance along the shore from Naples and close to the ruins of Pompeii are the remains (discovered in 1711) of what in ancient times was the thriving Roman town of Herculaneum. Herculaneum was first mentioned by the Greek writer Theophrastus in the latter part of the 4th century B.C., but it is believed to have existed long before. The town is known to have been attacked and conquered by the Samnites late in the 5th century B.C. It participated in the Social War against the power of Rome, was subdued, and became a Roman municipality in 89 B.C.

Like its neighbor, Pompeii, Herculaneum was severely damaged by an earthquake in 62 A.D. Both survived, only to meet destruction together from the violent eruption of Mount Vesuvius in 79 A.D. The circumstances were, however, quite different. Pompeii fell under a rain of hot ashes and cinders; Herculaneum was completely buried by a flood of mud which flowed down the mountainside. Because of this, the surface of the bells excavated at Herculaneum were found, in many cases, but not all, to be quite smooth, with the original patina still on many of them. Fortunately, because of the manner of Herculaneum's destruction, archaeologists were also able to bring to light in a comparatively good state of preservation the marvelous frescoes which adorned the walls of its public buildings and private dwellings. Like the bell in Figure 215 found at Pompeii, the bell from Herculaneum, illustrated in Figure 221, probably once hung from the neck of a bovid.

The Romans at Herculaneum

221

The Romans at Lake Nemi The bronze bells shown in Figures 222–227 were excavated at the site of the Temple of Diana, not far from the small medieval Italian town of Nemi and near the northeastern end of the lake which bears the town's name. The temple was erected by the Romans on an elevated spot in a sacred grove surrounded by a colonnade and commanded a fine view of the lake, sometimes referred to as the "Mirror of Diana" because of its clear, smooth surface. The temple is known to have existed until the 1st century B.C. Today, only its foundations remain; the colonnade is gone, but in the background a few niches still stand in crumbling condition. However, long before the Romans came into power the Italic people began construction of a temple on the same site.

The bells may be dated from about the 3rd to the 1st century B.C. Probably, all these bells formerly had been worn as articles of personal adornment or had hung from the necks of domestic animals. From time to time worshippers brought the bells to the temple as votive offerings. Such offerings customarily were sorted by attendants and placed in depositories, known as *stipes votivae*. Offerings of value were kept in one depository, while gifts of food were allocated to another. Objects of little intrinsic value, including personal belongings, were dumped into depositories dug in the ground at various spots within the sacred enclosure around the temple.

In some of the last-named, termed "ditches" (*favissae*) by archaeologists, several bells were found. The small bell in Figure 224 definitely is Punic and is similar in form to the four Punic bells discovered on the island of Ibiza, Spain, and portrayed in Figure 165. Unlike many Roman bells with clappers suspended from rings, this bell at one time contained a clapper which hung from a horizontal bar within the body of the bell. Holes for the bar are clearly visible.

The period to which the Roman bells and the single Punic bell in Figures 222–227 may be attributed encompassed about two hundred years, during which occurred Rome's decisive victory over the Carthaginians at Zama in 202 B.C., the end of the Second Punic War (218–201 B.C.), and the creation of a Roman province on African soil. The author believes that the Punic bell may have been among the personal possessions of a Roman legionnaire returning home from the African campaign.

Figures 222–227. Bronze bells. Lake Nemi, Italy. Roman Period, 3rd–1st century B.C. *222: height 6 cm. (2⅜ in.), diameter 4.5 cm. (1¾ in.). Patina light green. 223: height 9.5 cm. (3¾ in.), diameter 6.5 cm. (2⁹⁄₁₆ in.). Patina black. 224: height 4 cm. (1⁹⁄₁₆ in.), diameter 3 cm. (1³⁄₁₆ in.). Patina light brown.*

225: height 7 cm. (2¾ in.), diameter 5.1 cm. (2 in.). Patina mottled light and dark brown. 226: height 4 cm. (1⁹⁄₁₆ in.), diameter 5.5 cm. (2³⁄₁₆ in.). Patina light brown. 227: height 5.1 cm. (2 in.), diameter 5.5 cm. (2³⁄₁₆ in.). Patina light green. Courtesy of the Museo Nazionale di Villa Giulia, Rome.

183

222–224

225–227

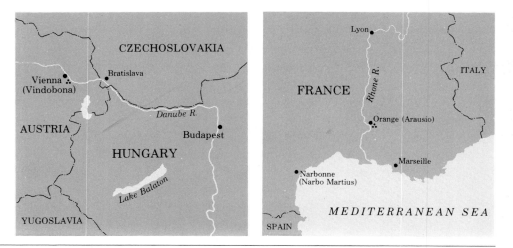

The Romans at Vienna

At the close of the 1st century B.C., the Romans, victorious over the Cimbrians and other Germanic tribes, gained their first foothold in the fertile lands along the Danube. A series of fortresses and fortified towns soon sprang up, as the Roman legions, and later Roman citizenry, occupied the conquered territory. One such fortress and seat of a provincial government was at Carnuntum. Not far from there, on a site of Celtic ancestry, the Romans under Emperor Claudius (10 B.C.–54 A.D.) established a permanent camp called Vindobona, the present-day Vienna.

Many Roman bells have been excavated in Vienna and its environs. Most were found without clappers. Since the clappers usually were made of iron, they rusted and disintegrated completely in damp soil.

The bell in Figure 228 is a rare exception—the clapper is in fine condition and swings freely on its suspension ring.

As for the bell in Figure 230, the clapper, somewhat corroded, has remained stuck to the bell's inner side, its escape prevented by the fact that the bell lay buried with its mouth pointing upward. The clapper looks like a caterpillar's cocoon.

The Romans at Orange

Roman bells excavated in France have proven to be identical in form to those unearthed at most Roman sites throughout Europe, Africa, and Asia Minor.

In Figure 231 appears an exquisitely cast bronze memorial found among the Roman ruins at Orange, a town of southern France in the province of Vaucluse. Orange became an important Roman colony in the 1st century A.D. The piece probably once hung in a sanctuary or in the household shrine of a private dwelling. At the top of the memorial is a bust of Mercury flanked left and right, respectively, by busts of helmeted Minerva and veiled Juno, resting upon cornucopias. Directly under the bust of Mercury appears the head of Jupiter.

Below are seven bronze bells hanging from individual chains. All the bells are ovoid except the center one, which is tetragonal. Their interiors are heavily corroded. All the clappers are missing. The patina of the entire memorial is greenish brown. A hole in the winged helmet of Mercury indicates that at one time a ring probably was attached there for use in suspending the memorial.

Figures 228–230. Bronze bells. Vienna, Austria. Roman Period, 1st–2nd century A.D. 228: height 4.2 cm. (1⅝ in.), diameter 4.4 cm. (1¾ in.). Patina light green. 229: height 7.3 cm. (2⅞ in.), diameter 4.8 cm. (1⅞ in.), depth 3.8 cm. (1½ in.). Patina dark brown. 230: height 5.4 cm. (2⅛ in.), diameter 5.7 cm. (2¼ in.). Patina dark green.

Figure 231. Bronze memorial with bells. Orange, France. Roman Period, 1st century A.D. Memorial: overall length 34 cm. (13⅜ in.), width 14 cm. (5¹⁷⁄₃₂ in.). Patina greenish brown. Bells: height 4.5 cm. (1¾ in.), diameter 3.2 cm. (1¼ in.). Patina greenish brown. Courtesy of the Bibliothèque Nationale, Paris.

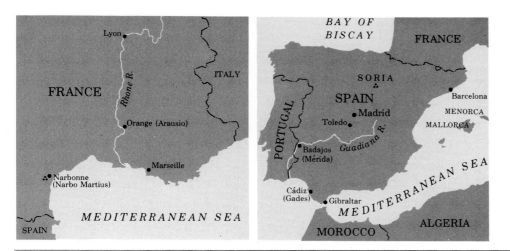

The Romans at Narbonne

Narbonne, France, ancient Narbo Martius, was colonized by the Romans in 116 B.C. No bells from Narbonne are reproduced in this book, but the Roman custom of hanging bells on dogs is well illustrated on a sandstone stela (1st century A.D.) the upper portion of which is shown in Figure 232. This funerary monument was erected over the graves of a miller, Marcus Careius Asisa, and his family.

The occupation of the *paterfamilias* is symbolized by the bas-relief of a millstone being turned by a donkey. To the right is a sarcophagus. Below rests the pathetic figure of a dog wearing a collar with a bell of the swinging-clapper type. For many centuries a dog has been regarded as a symbol of domestic fidelity.

The Visigoths

The Goths were one of a number of Germanic tribes regarded by the Romans as "barbarians" and with whom they came into conflict early in the 1st century A.D. Periodic warfare brought at various times, defeat and victory to each. In 270 A.D., during a brief period of peace, Emperor Aurelian (reigned 270–275) ceded lands to the Goths in Dacia (present-day Rumania). Those who settled in the western part were named Visigoths (West Goths); those in the eastern part, Ostrogoths, (East Goths). For a while, the Visigoths were staunch allies of the Romans. But by the beginning of the 5th century the Visigoths again were fighting Rome, and in 410 A.D. their king, Alaric, captured and sacked the city. In the previous year, the Vandals, Alani, and Suevi had overrun Iberia (Spain). By 415, the Visigoths once more had made peace with the Romans, and were able to move into Spain to bolster their shaky rule there. Under King Euric the Visigoths succeeded in defeating the Vandals, Alani, and Suevi between 466 and 483. Meanwhile, Rome fell in 476. Soon after the middle of the 6th century the Visigoths gained domination of the entire Iberian Peninsula. From their capital, Toledo, the Visigoths ruled until 711, when Roderick, their last king, was defeated and slain by the Moors under Tarik.

The bells left by the Visigoths are among the rarest excavated anywhere in the world. The author has been able to locate but one such bell (Figure 233). It is of bronze and was found in grave No. 6 of a 5th to 6th century A.D. necropolis in Soria Province, Spain. The bell probably was buried as a funerary gift.

188

Figure 232. Detail, sandstone stela.
Narbonne, France. Roman Period, 1st
century A.D. Width 85.1 cm. (33½ in.).
Courtesy of the Musée d'Art et
d'Histoire, Narbonne.

Figure 233. Bronze bell. Soria Province,
Spain. Visigothic Period, 5th–6th cen-
tury A.D. Height 5.1 cm. (2 in.), diam-
eter 2.5 cm. (1 in.). Patina dark brown.
Courtesy of the Museo Arqueológico
Nacional, Madrid.

233

Africa

*Figures 234 and 235. Bronze bell.
Egypt. Late Ptolemaic Period, 3rd–2nd
century B.C. Height 4.4 cm. (1¾ in.),
diameter 3.2 cm. (1¼ in.). Patina very
dark brown.*

*Plate 17 (p. 193) and Figure 239.
Bronze bell. Egypt. XXVIth Dynasty,
663–525 B.C. Height 6 cm. (2⅜ in.),
diameter 4.6 cm. (1¹³⁄₁₆ in.). Patina
light green.*

234

235

239

Egypt Many of the bells of ancient Egypt display an artistry greatly influenced by a religion in which the deification of animals played a most important part.

In Figures 234 and 235 is shown a small bronze bell of the Late Ptolemaic Period which may be dated from the 3rd to the 2nd century B.C. On its exterior protrude the heads of four deities, three of which are animals, namely: Khnum, the ram; Sekhmet, the lioness; and Anubis, the jackal; the fourth is the demigod Bes. The bell has a smooth surface with a very dark brown patina. The clapper is missing, but directly above the effigy of Sekhmet is a hole for a wire to hold a clapper. Somewhat similar in form is the bronze bell shown in Figure 236. It bears the head of the sacred bull, Apis. It is also of the Late Ptolemaic Period and may be dated from the 3rd to the 2nd century B.C.

It is believed that both of the aforementioned bells were worn as amulets. Pliny the Elder (23–79 A.D.), who visited Egypt in his travels, said that it was the custom there around 800–700 B.C. to wear bells as amulets. It is known that about the same period, which included virtually the entire XXIIIrd Dynasty (745–718 B.C.), it became the practice of parents to locate their wandering children by the tinkle of bronze bells on iron bracelets worn by the little ones. This custom was continued far into Egyptian history, and many such articles of adornment have been excavated from graves of the Roman and Coptic periods. Mention of the similar use of a bell has been made in connection with the Iberian bronze bell suspended from a child's bracelet illustrated in Figure 213.

The bronze bell portrayed in Figure 238 is characterized by the presence of a stylistic palm ornamentation resting upon a rectangular platform atop the bell's crown. A small hole is present for suspension purposes. The bell is of the Late Ptolemaic-Early Roman Period and dates from the second half of the 1st century B.C.

In contrast to the horses wearing bells depicted on various stone bas-reliefs in Assyrian palaces, horses portrayed on Egyptian bas-reliefs carry none. For example, no bells appear on the limestone carving from the Pyramid of Cheops, IVth Dynasty, one of the treasures of The Metropolitan Museum of Art in New York. Another excellent example, but of a much later period,

194

Figure 236. Bronze bell. Egypt. Late Ptolemaic Period, 3rd–2nd century B.C. Height 4.3 cm. (1 1/16 in.), diameter 3.5 cm. (1 3/8 in.). Patina brown. Courtesy of The Metropolitan Museum of Art, Gift of Miss Lily Place, 1923.

Figure 237. Bronze bell. Faiyûm, Egypt. Late Period, circa 850 B.C. Height 6 cm. (2 3/8 in.), diameter 5.7 cm. (2 1/4 in.). Patina light green. Courtesy of the Trustees of The British Museum, London.

Figure 238. Bronze bell. Egypt. Late Ptolemaic–Early Roman Period, second half of 1st century B.C. Height 5.1 cm. (2 in.), width 2.9 cm. (1 1/8 in.), depth 2.9 cm. (1 1/8 in.). Patina dark green.

240

241

238

237

236

Figure 240. Faience bell. Egypt. Late Ptolemaic Period, 3rd–1st century B.C. *Height 3 cm. (1³/₁₆ in.), diameter 2.5 cm. (1 in.). Pale greenish blue faience.*

Figure 241. Clay bell. Jebel Moya, Egypt (Sudan). Circa 750 B.C. *Height 4.1 cm. (1⅝ in.), diameter 3.5 cm. (1³/₈ in.). Patina grayish. Courtesy of the Trustees of The British Museum, London.*

illustrating the absence of bells on Egyptian horses, is a painted wooden chest housed in the National Museum in Cairo. This object was found at Thebes in the tomb of an XVIIIth Dynasty king, Tutankhamen (circa 1355 B.C.), and shows that monarch waging battle from a war chariot drawn by two horses. Nor are any to be seen upon the pylons of various Egyptian temples where King Ramses II (circa 1292–1225 B.C.) stands in his horse-drawn chariot, engaged in battle against the Hittites and other foes. Plate 17 (p. 193) and Figure 239 display a bronze effigy bell in the form of the head of Bes—the monstrous, bandy-legged, dwarfish demigod whose oracle was consulted at Abydos and who was popularly worshipped as guardian of the marriage chamber and protector of women in childbirth. Above the heavy eyebrows of his grotesque face rises a crown of feathers flanked by two tiny lizards facing forward. The bell, which is of the XXVIth Dynasty (663–525 B.C.), has a smooth surface covered by a light green patina. In place of the conventional suspension ring is a pierced disk, cast with the bell. It extends vertically, directly behind the feathered crown. High inside the bell remains a fragment of its corroded clapper.

Figure 240 shows a small, pale greenish-blue faience bell. There is a minute hole in the crown for the suspension of a clapper, now missing. This bell is of the Late Ptolemaic Period and may be dated from the 3rd to the 1st century B.C.

Bells in Egypt were worn by and frequently buried with favorite domestic animals, such as cows and sheep. The cowbells were of the swinging-clapper type, while those for sheep were crotals. Both varieties were of bronze.

Egyptians never placed bells at the necks of sacred cows or sacred bulls, to which godlike qualities were attributed. Clear evidence of this is shown on a fresco in the tomb of Queen Nefret-ere Mi-en-Mut, wife of Ramses II, located in the hills beyond the west bank of the Nile, opposite Thebes; there, the absence of bells is noted in the portrayal in vivid colors of seven sacred cows and one sacred bull; nor were bells placed upon other venerated animals, such as apes, cats, and falcons, represented in both sculptures and murals.

The bronze bell in Figure 237 was found in the Faiyum district and is of the Late Period, about 850 B.C. It has a round suspension

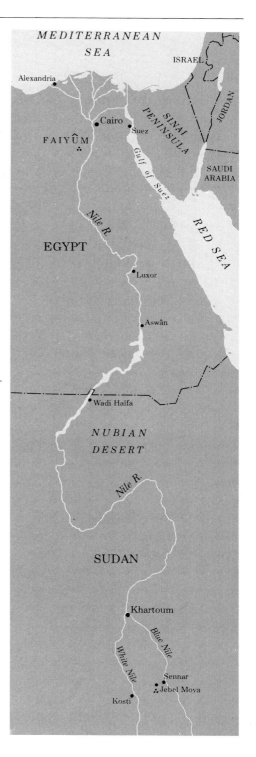

ring and is characterized by an unusually wide flare at its mouth. A heavy incrustation of soil covers the entire outer surface.

The clay bell shown in Figure 241 may be dated about 750 B.C. It is of grayish color and unglazed. The bell was found at Jebel Moya in the Sudan, south of Khartoum, at a site in the Gezira plain between the Blue Nile and the White Nile, by the Sir Henry Wellcome Expedition (1910–14). It was discovered in a grave during the first season of digging, in January 1911. The bell is one of only two pottery bells found at Jebel Moya. What may have been fragments of bells, but not recognized as such, were unearthed there too. Because of its fragile nature, the bell probably cannot be regarded as a child's toy, but rather as an amulet for an adult, a votive offering, or an object used in a religious ceremony.

Nigeria In 1938 archaeologists were very much excited by the news of the accidental discovery of a hoard of unusual ancient bronzes of artistic merit in Igbo-Ukwu, a town in Onitsha Province in eastern Nigeria. It is believed that various bronze objects had been found in a nearby area as early as 1922, though scientific excavations had never been undertaken. The bronzes found in 1938 and subsequently in the same locale have been judged to be about one thousand years old.

To distinguish the sites of the 1938 finds, they were named "Igbo Isaiah," "Igbo Jonah," and "Igbo Richard," after the first names of three members of the Anozie family, who were their owners.

In 1939 additional finds were made, and in 1944 the leaded bronze bell shown in Figure 242 was collected, presumably at Igbo Isaiah, by Kenneth Murray, Surveyor of Antiquities for the Nigerian Federal Department of Antiquities. The bell is conical with a circular suspension ring cast as part of the bell. Below it is a thin, false filigree coil which takes some dozen or more turns as it extends down over approximately one quarter of the bell's surface. Two additional lines enclose a series of dots running around the bell. The rest of its body displays chevrons arranged in four parallel groups running around the bell. Each chevron is trifold, with two narrow sections enclosing a broad one, and is punctuated at its extremities by bosses. Covering the rest of the

Figure 242. Leaded bronze bell. Igbo-Ukwu, eastern Nigeria. Circa 1000 A.D. Height 7.4 cm. (2¹⁵⁄₁₆ in.), diameter 4.1 cm. (1⅝ in.). Courtesy of the Department of Archaeology, University of Ibadan, Ibadan, Nigeria.

bell's surface are myriads of minute granules. At the mouth of the bell runs a ring of circular section.

In the same year, 1944, Murray collected the two very small crotals shown in Figures 245 and 246, which presumably also came from Igbo Isaiah. The bells were not analyzed, but they too appear to be of leaded bronze. They differ from each other in size and vary slightly in design. The bell in Figure 245 has four spiral bosses on each side of its suspension ring; the one in Figure 246 has three. Their domes, like the bosses, are spiral and terminate below in crescent-shaped mouths of circular section. The pellets are missing.

During 1959 and 1960 extensive excavations were carried out at Igbo-Ukwu by the Nigerian Federal Department of Antiquities and in 1964 by the Institute of African Studies, University of Ibadan, Nigeria, under the direction of Dr. C. Thurston Shaw, noted American archaeologist and head of the Department of Archaeology at the University of Ibadan. Among the hundreds of important objects discovered and collected by Dr. Shaw and his associates were several bronze bells of both swinging-clapper and crotal types. Some crotals are attached to chains formed of wire-twisted links, probably of copper. All of the crotals have the same flattened crescent form as those shown in Figures 245 and 246. The treasures included 21,784 pieces of pottery, more than 165,000 beads, scores of knives for household use, a vast number of bronze and copper ritual vessels, ceremonial objects and regalia, and numerous articles of personal adornment such as pendants, anklets, wristlets, and breastplates. Included also were many fragments of textiles, and weapons in the form of ornate bronze hilts and scabbards.

Concerning the culture of the bells discovered at Igbo-Ukwu the question arises whether they were cast locally or some distance away, even as far off as a thousand miles. Dr. Shaw offers the following general estimate: ". . . in spite of the distinctive character of the Igbo-Ukwu bronze work, it forms part of the West African bronze and brass casting continuum and was made east of the river Niger and south of the river Benue."

The bell shown in Figure 243 was presumably discovered at Igbo Isaiah or Igbo Jonah in 1964. Though not analyzed, it is probably leaded bronze. The bell departs from a truly cylindrical

242

Figure 243. Leaded bronze bell. Igbo-Ukwu, eastern Nigeria. Circa 1000 A.D. Height 13.7 cm. (5⅜ in.), diameter, top 8.1 cm. (3³⁄₁₆ in.), bottom 9.1 cm. (3⁹⁄₁₆ in.). Courtesy of the Department of Archaeology, University of Ibadan, Ibadan, Nigeria.

Figure 244. Leaded bronze bell. Igbo-Ukwu, eastern Nigeria. Circa 1000 A.D. Height 14.9 cm. (5⅞ in.), maximum width 11.7 cm. (4⅝ in.) (distortion), diameter at top 8.1 cm. (3³⁄₁₆ in.), estimated original diameter at bottom 9.1 cm. (3⁹⁄₁₆ in.). Courtesy of the Department of Archaeology, University of Ibadan, Ibadan, Nigeria.

243

244

Figures 245 and 246. Leaded bronze bells. Igbo-Ukwu, eastern Nigeria. Circa 1000 A.D. 245: height 2.2 cm. (⅞ in.). 246: height 1.9 cm. (¾ in.). Courtesy of the Department of Archaeology, University of Ibadan, Ibadan, Nigeria.

form in having a flaring crown and mouth, and thereby presents a graceful profile. Its flat circular top has a broad flange which extends obliquely upward. The suspension loop is strap-shaped. In the top of the bell, directly under the suspension loop, is a round hole through which a wire probably passed for hanging a clapper, now missing. Surrounding the suspension loop and set equidistantly apart are three concentric circles of sixteen bosses each. These are connected in low relief by a pattern of delicate crisscross lines and small dots resembling strings of beads. The pattern was lost in spots during the casting process. The outside surface of the bell is divided into four distinct zones. The upper zone occupies about half of it and carries a pattern similar to that on the top of the bell. Of the three zones below, the top and bottom each show four concentric circles of very small dots running around the bell, while the center zone, separated from the other two by fine lines and about twice as wide as either of them, is plain. The bell's mouth is bordered by a ring of ovoid section.

245

The leaded bronze bell in Figure 244 was also collected at Igbo Isaiah or Igbo Jonah in 1964. It was found in badly crushed condition, its shape almost reduced to two flattened and broken surfaces. Originally, the body of the bell undoubtedly was circular and its top was round and flat. The top bears an overall elevated design of nine small crotals arranged in a circle, their suspension rings facing inward toward the twisted, rope-shaped suspension ring of the bell itself. A flange projecting obliquely runs around the top of the bell. The bell's body displays at its top and bottom bands composed of concentric rings of small irregular dots. The mouth of the bell is framed by a ring of round section. Two sprue marks are visible on the top of the bell, and one each on the top of the handle and its lower edge. An explanation of sprue marks on bells is given in connection with the two bronze bells excavated in Argentina (Figures 304 and 305).

246

North America

The North American Indians

Widely divergent opinions have been offered by anthropologists and other scientists concerning the eastward movement of Asiatic people from Siberia across the land bridge to their first foothold upon the North American continent. Some believe that this occurred about 12,000 years ago; others say 20,000; some 30,000; and some say even earlier. There is archaeological evidence to support some of their beliefs. Man's initial immigration, however, did not take the form of a mass movement; on the contrary, it was characterized by gradual infiltrations of small groups of gatherers and hunters who wandered into lands where animal life abounded. Anthropologists and historians have deduced from their studies of glacial history that there were two long, separate periods when a land bridge permitted man to cross over on foot from the eastern headlands of Siberia to the western coast of Alaska.

On the basis of archaeological discoveries and glacial geology they have calculated that the first of those periods occurred between about 28,000 and 23,000 B.C.; and the second, between about 14,000 and 10,000 B.C. As the ice melted at the close of the latter period, the sea level rose and formed the Bering Strait; the land bridge disappeared beneath its waters, and further Asian migrations to the Western Hemisphere, except by water, were cut off. Having penetrated the continent's ice barriers, man moved southward. The new population increased as it migrated, at the same time fanning out both to the east and to the west over an unpeopled continent, the rich potential of which awaited exploitation. As time passed, the descendants of America's first inhabitants, later called Indians, altered their way of life; once exclusively hunters and gatherers, they now became tillers of the soil as well.

History, millennia later, was to witness throughout the Western Hemisphere the evolvement of some of the world's greatest cultures and the creation of some of its most interesting and beautiful bells.

Almost hidden from view under overhanging cliffs in the states of Arizona, Colorado, New Mexico, and Utah lie crumbling ruins, the former abodes of Indians generally referred to as "Cliff Dwellers." Though some anthropologists believe that the Spanish were aware of the existence of Indian ruins in the Southwest, our

Figures 247 and 248. Clay bell fragment. Luna County, New Mexico. Mogollon, Mimbres Culture, circa 1050–1200 A.D. Height 3.7 cm. (1⁷⁄₁₆ in.), width 2.6 cm. (1 in.). Color reddish brown. Courtesy of the Museum of New Mexico, Sante Fe.

first knowledge of the inhabitants there came in 1874 with the chance discovery of an Indian ruin in Mancos Canyon, Colorado, by William H. Jackson, the well-known photographer associated with a U.S. government geological and geographical survey of the surrounding territory. During the ensuing years more Indian cliff dwellings in other canyon walls were discovered. In prehistoric times they had sheltered the ancestors of the Indians found by the invading Spaniards, who later gave them the name "Pueblos." In general, three major prehistoric Pueblo cultures are now recognized in the Southwest: the Hohokam in southern Arizona, showing Mexican influence; the Mogollon in southwestern New Mexico; and the renowned Anasazi. Ruins of the last-named are scattered over the "four corners," the area where the present states of Arizona, New Mexico, Colorado, and Utah meet. The art of basketry became highly developed among the Anasazi, and the name "Basket Makers" has been applied to their culture from the start of the 1st century A.D., long before they learned of pottery from the Mogollon. The latter had been making fired pottery since the 1st century A.D., but not until about 700 A.D. did the Anasazi practice this craft. However, few entire clay bells have been excavated, and even fragmentary ones are rare.

247

From the Mimbres Culture of the Mogollon is the reddish-brown clay bell shown in Figures 247 and 248, ascribed to the period 1050–1200 A.D. It was discovered in Luna County, near the southwestern corner of New Mexico. It is only a fragment; almost half of the bell is missing, as well as the pellet. Smudging, carbonization, and cordage marks are clearly visible on the inside wall. Its upper section is arched and it is pierced with a hole for suspension. The hole shows slight signs of wear.

The American archaeologist Norton Allen, who was working with the Museum of New Mexico in 1953, gave the following description of how such a bell was made: "A sphere of clay for the clapper was placed within a ball of cotton textile or, perhaps, another substance covered with cloth and then wrapped with a few turns of string. Around this the bell was fashioned. Firing consumed the material within, leaving the clapper in place." (What Norton Allen terms a "clapper" in his description of the making of a crotal-type clay bell is called a "pellet" throughout

248

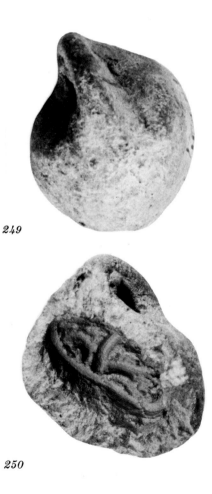

249

250

this book, differentiating it from the swinging clapper of an open-mouthed bell.)

In Figures 249 and 250 the upper portion of a light tan clay bell of the Anasazi culture is portrayed. It has a loop handle. Rough tool marks are visible within its hollow interior. The bell dates from the 17th century A.D. and was found in the Cuyamungue Pueblo near Tesuque, New Mexico, by Helen Warren in 1972.

Some anthropologists believe that probably before 14,000 B.C., and definitely by 9000 B.C., several migrating tribes had reached what is now the eastern United States, where their descendants eventually produced the Adena/Hopewell and "Mississippian" cultures. On the Tennessee River in northern Alabama the Copena culture, which might be regarded as a variant of Hopewell, emerged. All these cultures produced mounds of earth that served as burial and ceremonial sites and as bases upon which could be built altars, temples, council houses, or dwellings. When the mounds were discovered by white inhabitants of the area during the 19th century, the name "Mound Builders" was given to their creators. Since man-made mounds have appeared through the ages in many parts of the world, there seems to be no more justification for applying the name to this American group than to others who erected mounds, such as the Scythians, who built kurgans, and the Etruscans, whose mounds are called tumuli. Once upon a time, thousands of mounds of various shapes and sizes dotted the landscape from the Great Lakes to the Gulf of Mexico, from the Atlantic to the Mississippi and beyond. Some were round, but in Wisconsin, Iowa, and Ohio were many "effigy mounds" in the clearly outlined forms of birds and animals: eagle, fox, turtle, bear, and others. Weather erosion, inexperienced diggers, and urban development have altered the shapes or totally destroyed many of these mounds. The most spectacular one still extant is undoubtedly the giant Serpent Mound. Its form approaches that of the horned or plumed serpent, one of the principal deities of many Indian tribes that inhabited lands as far south as present-day Central America. The mound is situated near the village of Locust Grove in Adams County, Ohio, on a site set apart as a public park and state memorial. Its creation has been attributed to the Adena culture, and it is believed to have been formed between 200 B.C. and 700 A.D.

Extensive excavations of burial mounds in the valleys of the
Ohio and Mississippi rivers have yielded a wealth of artifacts.
There are few mounds in the United States which have given forth
as many artifacts and human skeletons as the King Mounds at
Wickliffe, Kentucky, located close to the confluence of the Ohio
and the Mississippi rivers. Those mounds were excavated by the
archaeologists Colonel Fain White King and his wife, Blanche
Busey King, between 1932 and 1939. In addition to human
skeletons and animal bones, the site yielded numerous bone and
stone artifacts, many shell, copper, and stone ornaments, and
quantities of beads. Included were flint spearpoints and
arrowheads, stone fetishes, clay figurines and potsherds.
Copper was brought down from Isle Royale in Lake Superior
and the surrounding area. Being malleable, it was easily
cold-hammered into tools and other objects, including beads.
The casting of metal was still an unknown art to the inhabitants
of the Ohio and upper Mississippi regions. No excavations of their
mounds or graves have ever yielded copper bells.
Among the thousands of objects unearthed at Wickliffe,
Kentucky, by Colonel and Mrs. King was the black clay bell
illustrated in Figure 251. It may be dated about 900 A.D. The
bell has a polished surface and contains a single clay pellet.
Opposite its mouth, but not visible in the photograph, are two small
holes, close to each other, through which threads of deer sinew
could be passed for stringing the bells or attaching them to fabric.
In a letter written in 1947, referring to clay bells, Colonel King
said, "We find them about the legs and above the feet, also often
around the neck."
The bell is similar in shape to some of the clay crotals of
Mexico which belong to that country's Pre-Classic Period.
While Indians north of them were still making such bells of
clay, the tribes of Mexico had progressed in metallurgy and were
beginning to cast bells and other objects by the lost-wax method.
Later, many Mexican bells, such as the teardrop-shaped copper
crotals of the Post-Classic Period, were brought north and through
trade reached many tribes of the North American Southwest.

251

Mexico The spherical, burnished clay bell in Figure 252 belongs to Mexico's Pre-Classic Period, which may be dated from about 2000 B.C. to the Christian era. Metallurgy reached Mexico about 900 A.D. It is interesting to note that the largest quantity of archaeological bells yet discovered at any one site in the world has come, not from "dry digs," but from underwater excavations at Chichén Itzá, in the state of Yucatán, a city already of great importance during the Mayan era. Several thousand copper bells and a small number of gold bells of the crotal type have been taken from a single site there, the "Sacred Well." Often referred to as the "Well of Sacrifice," but called Chen Ku ("Sacred Well)" by the Mayas and El Cenote by the Mexicans, this pool is almost circular and measures 180 feet (55 meters) in diameter. In spots it has a depth of 55 feet (17 meters). It is fed by underground springs. For more than 800 years this small body of water was one of the most venerated spots in the Western Hemisphere, attracting Mayan pilgrims from all parts of Meso-America. It continued to draw worshippers throughout the days of the Mayas' conquerors, the Toltecs, as well as during the Maya-Toltec Period (987–1224 A.D.). In Colonial times it contributed to the belief that Chichén Itzá was as sacred to the Indians as Mecca is to the Moslems and Rome to the Christians. Meager ruins of a small Mayan temple stand at one spot where the ground ends abruptly and overlooks the still surface of the water below—a sheer drop of some 70 feet (21 meters). Tons of this temple's stones, which in the course of the years fell into the Well, have been recovered from its muddy bottom. Close by the ruins, the evidence of an altar dedicated to the Mayan rain god, Chac, still remains; from a platform facing that altar the Mayas carried out their elaborate ceremonies of human sacrifice. The Mayas believed that the wrath of Chac had to be appeased each time a drought occurred, presenting the threat of famine. To gain Chac's favor and obtain rain for their sun-baked fields of maize, the Mayas offered as sacrifices their most cherished possessions— their young sons and virgin daughters. While musicians provided accompaniment to the chanting of the worshippers and the air was filled with perfumed smoke rising from clay pots of burning copal (resin obtained from the pom tree), a victim, heavily weighted down and richly bedecked with bells, stone beads, and

252

Figure 252. Clay bell. Mexico. Pre-Classic Period, circa 2000 B.C.–Christian Era. Diameter 2.4 cm. ($^{15}/_{16}$ in.). Color dark gray.

other prized articles of adornment, would be brought forward by two colorfully attired priests and thrown alive, clear of the altar's edge, into the Sacred Well.

This, at least, has been the accepted version of the Mayan ceremony at the Sacred Well. In televised lectures delivered in 1975, however, the late British archaeologist Sir Eric Thompson (1899–1975) presented another interpretation. He declared that the Mayas did not throw their own children into the Well. He claimed that there was a regular trade in young orphans and that there were markets where Mayan parents could purchase a child to keep until the time came when a need, such as a drought, made them wish to offer a human sacrifice. It is noteworthy that more than half of all the skulls brought up from the Well were of children between the ages of eight months and twelve years.

The majority of the bells recovered were votive offerings tossed into the Well by pilgrims; the remainder came from the necklaces, bracelets, and garments of human sacrifices. Most bells are of pure copper or of copper alloyed with tin or lead; silver often was present in such bells but only as an impurity. Some were of *tumbaga*, a low-grade gold, some of gold-plated copper, and a very limited number of solid gold. The solid-gold bells generally were of the Cocle Province or Veraguas Province types from Panama. There also were bells made by the *mise en couleur* method—alloying copper with a lesser amount of gold. Sometimes, small amounts of other metals were included. However, the presence of gold was essential. To obtain a gold surface on the bell an acid believed to have come from the juice of a plant was applied. This ate away the copper on the bell's surface and left the gold, which was then polished. The process could be repeated later to produce a similar result. In carrying out the process of gold-plating bells, whether or not they contained gold as an alloy, gold was introduced from the outside and applied directly to the bell's surface.

The Mayas, highly skilled in many arts and crafts, ostensibly had no knowledge whatsoever of metallurgy. The bells they themselves brought to the Well were acquired chiefly through trade with their neighbors. Bells served as a ready medium of exchange throughout the Americas. The author has not seen any bells from the Well of the swinging-clapper variety and he believes that all the bells recovered have been of the crotal type—

Figure 253. Gold-plated copper bell. Chichén Itzá, Yucatán, Mexico. Veraguas Style, circa 12th century A.D. Height 4.2 cm. (1⅝ in.). Courtesy of the Peabody Museum, Harvard University.

Plate 18 (p. 209). Gold-plated copper bell. Chichén Itzá, Yucatán, Mexico. Veraguas Style, circa 12th century A.D. Height 8.4 cm. (3 3/16 in.). Courtesy of the Peabody Museum, Harvard University.

Figure 254. Copper bells. Chichén Itzá, Yucatán, Mexico. Post-Classic Period, circa 1000–1520 A.D. Top row: height (largest) 3 cm. (1 3/16 in.). Middle row: height (largest) 2.5 cm. (1 in.). Bottom row: height (largest) 1.5 cm. (⅝ in.). Patina dark brown. Courtesy of the Peabody Museum, Harvard University.

Figure 255. Copper bells. Chichén Itzá, Yucatán, Mexico. Post-Classic Period, circa 1000–1520 A.D. Top row: height (largest) 3.8 cm. (1½ in.). Middle row: height (largest) 3.8 cm. (1½ in.). Bottom row: height (largest) 2.9 cm. (1⅛ in.). Patina dark brown. Courtesy of the Peabody Museum, Harvard University.

253

the majority pear-shaped or spherical. Few of the bells recovered from the Well contained pellets. It appears that before many of the copper bells (Figures 254, 255, and 256) were thrown into the Well, their pellets were removed, generally causing little or no damage to the bells, but silencing them forever. However, the absence of pellets does not necessarily mean that the pellets were removed by their devout owners. Many bells may have been thrown into the Well in perfect condition, but long submersion may have caused the pellets, especially those made of clay, to disintegrate. Some bells with extremely wide mouths were never made with the intention that they should hold pellets. Originally they had been sewn closely together upon garments or leg bands, where any movement of the wearer caused them to strike against one another and produce rattling sounds. Often some pious individuals, acting in the same spirit which motivated them to sacrifice human lives, "killed" their bells by going to the extreme of smashing them flat, or nearly so. An example of such a practice is seen in the gold-plated copper bell in Plate 18 (p. 209), recovered from the Well by the Harvard University Peabody Museum Expedition of 1907–10, under the direction of Edward H. Thompson. This bell has been badly crushed, but the suspension ring on its platform is intact. Against it, in a vertical position, rests the form of a parrot displaying its claws and upturned tail. Another gold-plated copper bell (Figure 253) found by that expedition has suffered considerably less damage—apparently at the hands of a devotee. It still contains a gold pellet. The platform supports the form of an eagle with outstretched wings. Another aquatic find of the 1907–10 expedition is the gold bell shown in Plate 20 (p. 213, top right). It has the form of a seated monkey which has two tails and holds one tail in each hand. At its back is a small suspension loop. The pellet is missing. Recovered from the Well at the same time were two other gold bells: the turtle in Plate 21 (p. 213, bottom right) and what appears to be a piglet eating an ear of corn in Plate 19 (p. 213 left). There is no pellet in the body of the former, but the latter contains one of gold. In 1910 the expedition brought up a copper bell (Figure 257) from the same watery grave. The bell represents a jaguar's head with squint eyes, small ears, and a short snout. It has a double suspension ring at the top. No pellet is present.

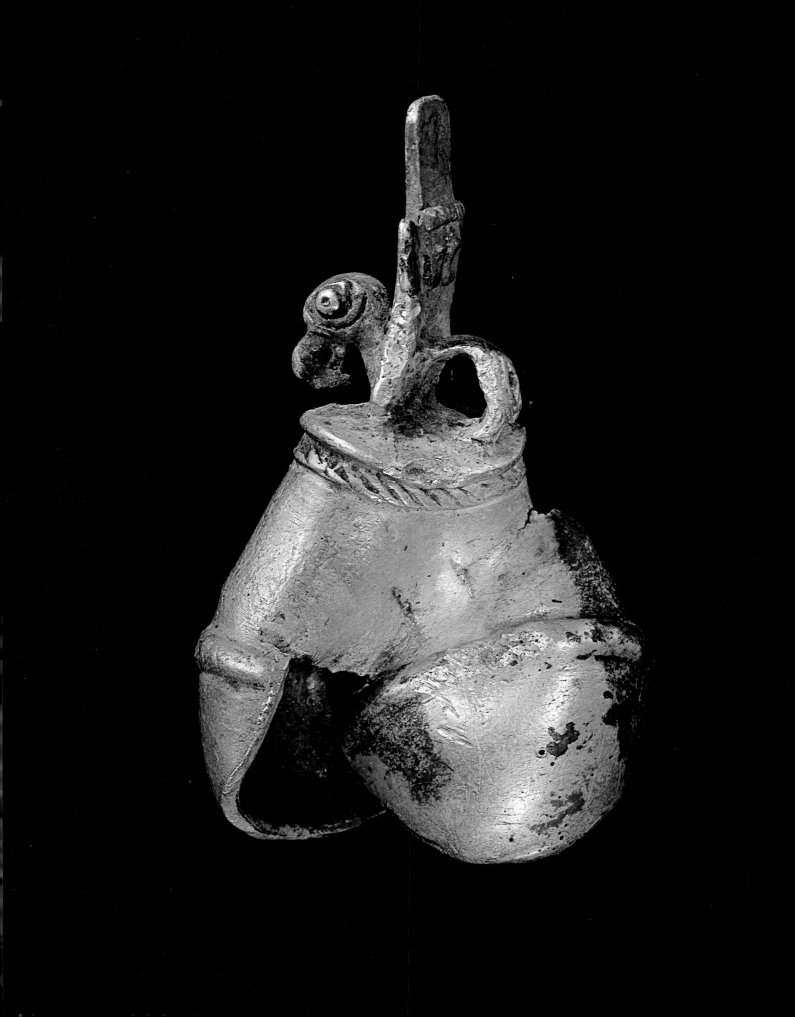

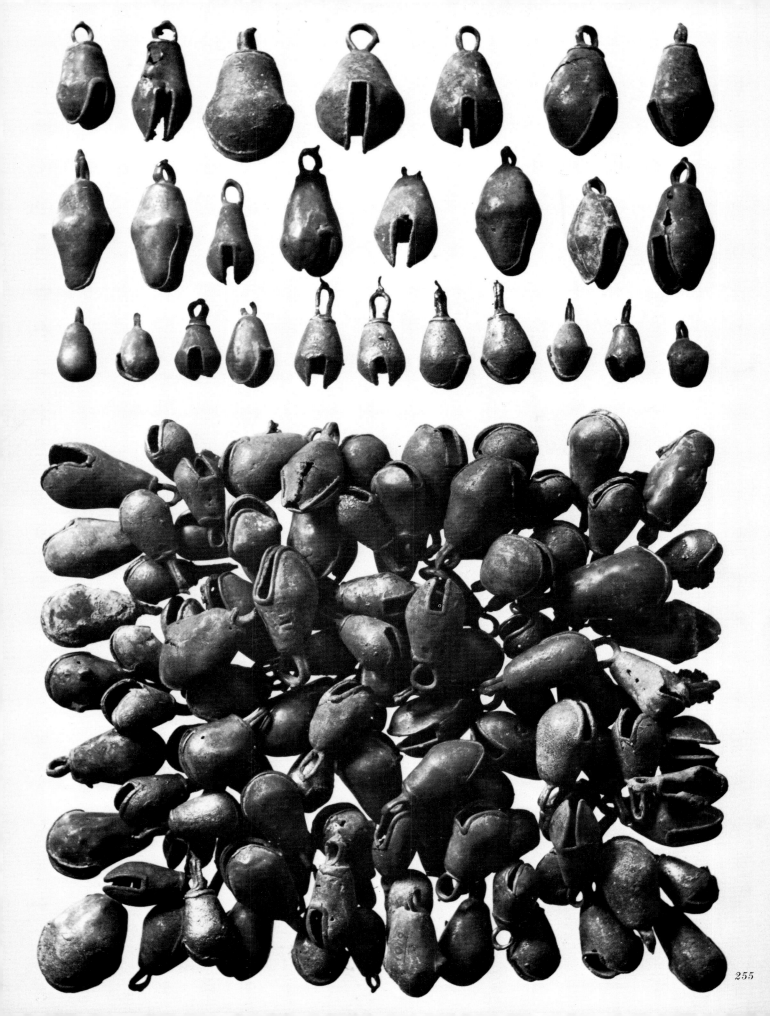

255

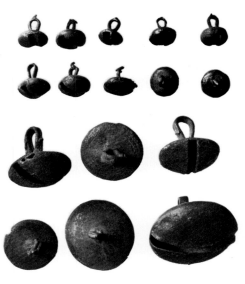

256

Among the many other bells that divers brought up from the Well were hundreds of small copper crotals with smooth surfaces, almost all devoid of pellets. These bells fall into three distinct groups according to their shapes: spherical ones (Figure 254), pear-shaped ones (Figure 255), and those of ellipsoidal form, closely resembling buttons (Figure 256). The lower sections of the last-named are slit entirely from one side to the other. All three types have suspension loops. In the pear-shaped bells, many of those loops rest upon circular platforms, examples of which are the first three and the last two portrayed in the top row of Figure 255. The mouths of some are elongated, resembling somewhat the tapering jaws of a crocodile, as exemplified by the first two bells at the left in the middle row. Both the spherical and the pear-shaped bells may be subdivided into two categories: those cast with plain lips, as illustrated by the spherical examples in Figure 256, and those cast with thickened lips, as shown by the pear-shaped ones in Figure 255. Very few of the bells contain pellets.

Figures 258–261 illustrate the author's conception of the various stages in the preparation of the model and mold in the lost-wax method of casting—in this case, the crotal-type, Late Post-Classic copper bell portrayed in Figure 263. The procedure was as follows: First, a jade bead (sometimes a stone pebble, or a metal or hard-baked clay pellet) was inserted in a lump of moist clay mixed with charcoal. This clay core was then given the general shape desired and dusted with pulverized charcoal. Following this, either a solid covering of beeswax was applied to give a flat, smooth surface to the model, or a very fine thread of wax was wound around and around the core, as upon a spool, to produce a ridged surface. In either case, the thickness of the wax coating determined the actual thickness of the completed bell.

At this point, a carved stone saddle was introduced. A section of the wax surface and a part of the core were cut out from the lower part of the model, producing a mouth for the bell of proper size to fit the stone saddle. Desired decorative effects were achieved by applying short lengths of wax thread to the model's outer surface. A loop for suspension, usually made of a single or double turn of wax thread, was also placed on top of it. The model was then set astride the stone saddle and its entire wax

257

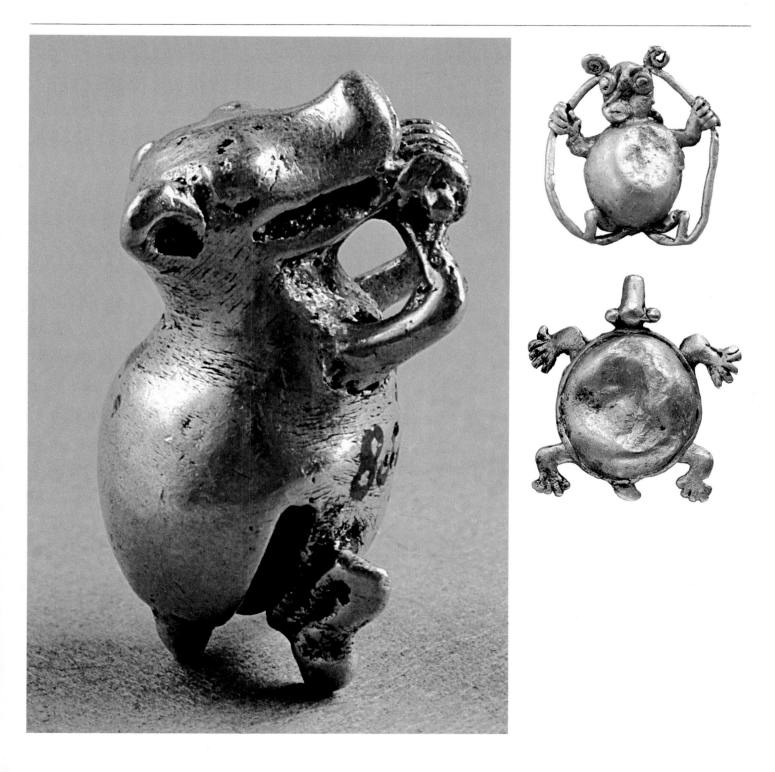

Plate 20 (p. 213 top right). Gold bell pendant. Chichén Itzá, Yucatán, Mexico. Coclé Style, circa 12th century A.D. Length 2.5 cm. (1 in.), weight 14 grams. Courtesy of the Peabody Museum, Harvard University.

Plate 21 (p. 213 bottom right). Gold bell pendant. Chichén Itzá, Yucatán, Mexico. Veraguas Style, circa 12th century A.D. Length 3.2 cm. (1¼ in.), weight 14.5 grams. Courtesy of the Peabody Museum, Harvard University.

Figures 258–261. Rendition of author's conception of model and mold used in the casting of a Mexican copper bell by lost-wax method.

Figure 262. Copper bells. State of Michoacán, Mexico. Post-Classic Period, circa 1000–1520 A.D. Average length 5.7 cm. (2¼ in.). Patina dark green.

Figure 263. Copper bell. State of Guerrero, Mexico. Post-Classic Period, circa 1000–1520 A.D. Length 7.6 cm. (3 in.). Patina light green.

258–261

surface sprinkled with charcoal dust. It was then covered by repeated coatings of fine, damp clay pressed firmly against its surface. A pouring duct was left in the top of the clay mass. When the clay covering was deemed thoroughly dry, a sufficient amount of heat was applied to melt the wax, which flowed out, leaving an impression within the mold. Molten metal was then poured into it, filling the impression previously occupied by the wax. After the metal had solidified and cooled, the mold was broken up, revealing the created bell. Lastly, the inside core was picked out in small particles through the bell's mouth, thus freeing the pellet and permitting it to roll about and produce the awaited sound.

High-ranking officials often wore bands with bells attached around the calves and occasionally around the ankles; sometimes these bands were of fur, but generally they were of cotton. In Figure 262 a small piece of cotton cloth still clings to the side of one of the four Michoacan copper bells in the central group, and a few maguey fibers remain wrapped about the suspension loops of two others.

The copper bell portrayed in Figure 263 was excavated in 1940 in the state of Guerrero. A representation of the sun with twelve rays appears in bold relief at one point on its surface. The remainder is covered with straight, crisscross, and zigzag lines and with spirals. The bell contains a single pale green jade bead. Such a bell and those shown in Figure 262 were cast during the Late Post-Classic Period (circa 1200–1550 A.D.) in both its Toltec and Aztec phases; they were found throughout southern Mexico from Michoacan to Yucatan and as far south as Honduras.

In Plate 22 (p. 216) appears a West Coast copper effigy bell of the Late Post-Classic Period. It is in the form of a human head wearing a cap. The septum is pierced and at one time may have held a nose ring. The bell contains one stone pellet.

A gold Mixtec bell, containing a green jade bead as a pellet, is portrayed in Plate 23 (p. 218). The bell's mouth lies between two cupped jaguar paws with realistically fashioned claws. Just above the paws and separated from them by a single twisted strand rest groups of other, simple strands, diagonally overlapping one another. Above them another twisted strand encircles a platform, in the center of which quadruple strands

263

262

Plate 22 (p. 216). Copper bell. West Coast, Mexico. Late Post-Classic Period, circa 1200–1550 A.D. Height 12.7 cm. (5 in.). Patina light brown. Courtesy of the Alvin Abrams Collection.

Figure 264. Copper bell. Champotón, Campeche, Mexico. Post-Classic Period, circa 1000–1520 A.D. Length 4.2 cm. (1⅝ in.). Patina light brown.

Figure 265. Copper bell. Champotón, Campeche, Mexico. Post-Classic Period, circa 1000–1520 A.D. Length 2.5 cm. (1 in.). Patina dark brown.

Figure 266. Copper bell. Chichén Itzá, Yucatán, Mexico. Post-Classic Period, circa 1000–1520 A.D. Height 1.9 cm. (¾ in.). Patina light brown. Courtesy of the Peabody Museum, Harvard University.

form a suspension loop. Except for the gold bells attached to the Aztec and Mixtec jewelry discovered at Monte Alban and Oaxaca, few gold bells of Mexican workmanship have been found. The copper bell in Figure 264 was found at Champoton in the state of Campeche. Its lower half is almost spherical; its upper half is composed of two pairs of vertical ribbons alternating with two others which terminate in reverse spirals. A double loop serves as a suspension ring. A considerable number of bells of somewhat similar design have been brought up from the bottom of the Sacred Well at Chichen Itza.

Also unearthed at Champoton was the copper bell in the form of a jaguar's head, illustrated in Figure 265. Each of the Champoton bells contains a copper pellet.

The copper bell in Figure 266 portrays the head of a monkey. It was found in the Well during excavations made by the 1904–7 Peabody Museum Expedition. It holds no pellet. Found at the same time was the copper bell shown in Figure 267. It is in the form of a human head and is without a pellet. The outlines of the eyes and of the rectangular mouth stand out in bold relief against the smooth surface of the other facial features. The two small protuberances which appear close together on the forehead are probably bits of metal which remained in the channels (sprues) of the clay mold and which customarily would be removed after the casting process was completed. Atop the bell is a double suspension ring.

The copper bell in Figure 268 is of the crotal type and represents a turtle. Its mouth is open and points straight upward. There is a narrow semicircular slit in the posterior section of its body. Two clay pellets are present. A suspension ring on the bell's flat bottom renders the object serviceable as a pendant.

Figure 269 depicts a pear-shaped copper bell from Michoacan. Its suspension ring rests upon a circular platform. Within the bell rolls a single clay pellet.

The Mixtec gold pendant in Plate 24 (p. 222) was found in the National Valley at Oaxaca. It is in the form of a stylized human skull with large bulging eyeballs. Narrow ribbon-like suspension loops, welded to the lower jaw, pass through narrow slits near the rear molar teeth of the upper jaw. This arrangement permits the lower jaw to open and close freely, as demonstrated in Figure 272.

264

265

266

Plate 23 (p. 218). Gold bell. Mexico. Mixtec Culture, circa 1500 A.D. Height 2.9 cm. (1⅛ in.), weight 11.27 grams.

Figure 267. Copper bell. Chichén Itzá, Yucatán, Mexico. Post-Classic Period, 1000–1520 A.D. Height 2.8 cm. (1⅛ in.). Patina dark gray. Courtesy of the Peabody Museum, Harvard University.

Figure 269. Copper bell. State of Michoacán, Mexico. Post-Classic Period, circa 1000–1520 A.D. Height 7.6 cm. (3 in.). Patina dark reddish brown.

Attached to the lower jaw are three rings. The one in the center is empty. From each of the other two hangs a small gold cylinder of openwork design with teardrop-shaped gold bells. The bells are without pellets.

The gold ring in Figure 270 was found in 1932 when an undisturbed Mixtec tomb of a high-ranking official was discovered at Monte Alban by one of Mexico's most celebrated archaeologists, Dr. Alfonso Caso. This tomb, which has yielded other exquisite gold jewelry, has been designated tomb No. 7. The ring was cast by the lost-wax method to present the appearance of filigree work. A rectangular plaque cast as part of the ring holds an eagle's head with feathered crown and other plumage, from which are suspended, at right and left, two gold teardrop-shaped bells without pellets. The eagle's beak holds a plaque of geometric form from which hang five gold bells, similar to the others, and all without pellets.

The gold Mixtec lip plug (labret) in Figure 271 was found at Monte Alban. The cylindrical section, which clearly protrudes below the lower lip when worn, terminates in an eagle's head. From its beak hangs a panel in the form of a stylized butterfly, supporting four links decorated with spirals. Below are suspended four spherical gold bells.

In Figures 273 and 274 appear two copper bells of the Late Post-Classic Period which were excavated in western Mexico; they are identical in form. Their broad suspension rings are gracefully arched across high cylindrical platforms boldly incised with crisscross designs. The bell in Figure 273 is in excellent condition, though no pellet is present. The lower part of the bell in Figure 274, however, has been badly crushed, undoubtedly an indication that it was intentionally "killed" by its pious owner— its "voice" destroyed forever.

Various stone sculptures and paintings depict deities and humans wearing bells as ornaments of personal adornment. Some of the finest examples of the latter art are to be found on the pages of pre-Conquest codices. However, the small size of the pages upon which the artists crowded many human figures, some of whom wore bells, precluded the possibility of showing either the exact shapes of the bells or their sizes in proportion to their wearers. On page 37 of the Mixtec *Codex Vindobonensis Mexicanus 1*

267

269

268

Figure 270. Gold ring. Monte Albán,
Mexico. Mixtec Culture, circa 1500 A.D.
Height 5.5 cm. (2³⁄₁₆ in.). Courtesy of
the Museo Nacional de Antropología,
Mexico, D.F.

Figure 271. Gold labret. Monte Albán,
Mexico. Mixtec Culture, circa 1500 A.D.
Length 5.5 cm. (2³⁄₁₆ in.). Courtesy of
the Museo Nacional de Antropología,
Mexico, D.F.

Plate 24 (p. 222) and Figure 272. Gold pendant with bells. National Valley, Oaxaca, Mexico. Mixtec Culture, circa 1500 A.D. Length 8.3 cm. (3¼ in.). Courtesy of the Museo Nacional de Antropología, Mexico, D.F.

Figure 273. Copper bell. Western Mexico. Late Post-Classic Period, circa 1200–1550 A.D. Length 11 cm. (4⁵⁄₁₆ in.). Patina green. Courtesy of the Museo Nacional de Antropología, Mexico, D.F.

Figure 274. Copper bell. Western Mexico. Late Post-Classic Period, circa 1200–1550 A.D. Length 9.5 cm. (3¾ in.). Patina green. Courtesy of the Museo Nacional de Antropología, Mexico, D.F.

Figures 275 and 276. Copper bells on hairpins. State of Michoacán, Mexico. Post-Classic Period, circa 1000–1520 A.D. 275: length 5.5 cm. (2³⁄₁₆ in.). 276: length 5.7 cm. (2¼ in.). Patina light green with heavy incrustations.

273

274

275-276

(Vienna Codex), a facsimile of which is shown in Figure 277, the artist has endeavored to portray the legend of the birth of the Mixtec people ("people of the clouds"), who lived in the mountainous region around Oaxaca.

The painting shows two round piles of ashes remaining upon the hard, stony ground after the world has been destroyed by fire. The only plant life that remains is a tree, the mesquite or honey locust; its branches bristle with pods, and minute curls adorn its bark. One half of the tree shows disks, the other arrows. The head of a goddess, face down, forms its roots, as she gives lifeblood to nourish the tree. At right and left, wearing spherical bells attached to bands above their wrists and just below their knees, stand two black-painted minor gods. Quetzal plumes connote their divine status. They engage their knives in an effort to carve out a drum from the tree's trunk. The trunk is split part of the way down the middle, its center giving birth first to a naked little woman and then a naked little man—the progenitors of the Mixtec people.

In Figures 275–276 are two delicately cast copper hairpins from Michoacan. They are of the Post-Classic Period. Their heads are in the form of bells, the pin in Figure 275 having one bell, the one in 276, two. The pellets which they once contained are missing.

The copper bell pendant shown in Figure 279 presents a lifelike representation of an armadillo, an animal venerated by many of the peoples of Meso-America and frequently cast in copper and in gold. This bell, found in western Mexico, is of the Late Post-Classic Period. There is a long narrow opening on its left side, just below its shell. Inside rolls a single pellet. On its right side are two small holes in the shell for a suspension cord.

Also of the Late Post-Classic Period is the clay bell in Figure 280. It is surmounted by the head of an old man wearing large earplugs. Passing from side to side through the figure's neck is a hole for a suspension cord.

Figure 278 portrays a pendant in the form of a turtle carrying a very small turtle on its back. Both turtle forms are bells. Only the larger one holds a pellet, clearly visible in the photograph. This object, of the Late Post-Classic Period, is of the Tarascan culture and was found in Michoacan. It has a suspension ring in a position similar to that of the ring on the bell in Figure 268.

Figure 277. Facsimile of page 37 of the Codex Vindobonensis Mexicanus I (Vienna Codex). Mexico. Mixtec Culture, circa 1000 A.D. Height 22.2 cm. (8¾ in.), length 26.7 cm. (10½ in.). Courtesy of the Peabody Museum, Harvard University.

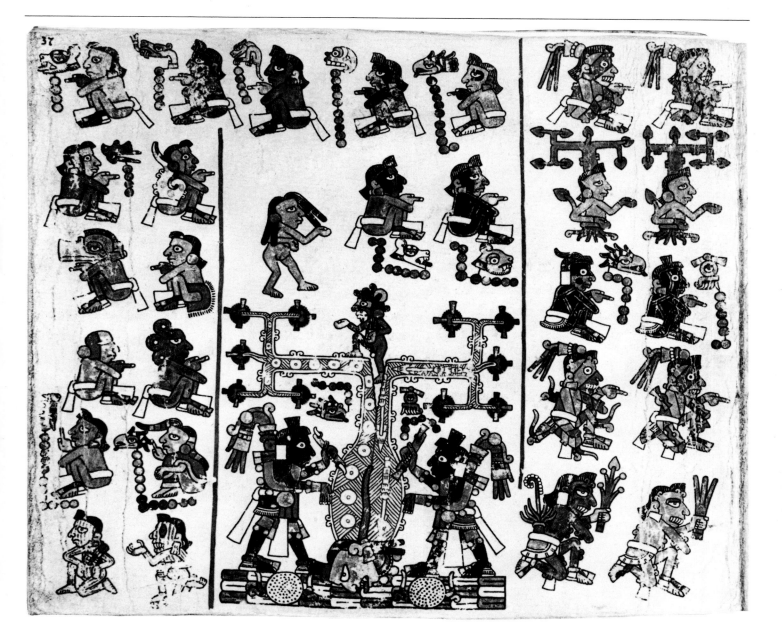

Figure 278. Copper bell pendant. State of Michoacán, Mexico. Late Post-Classic Period, circa 1200–1550 A.D. Length 8.9 cm. (3½ in.). Patina dark brown. Courtesy of the Museo Nacional de Antropología, Mexico, D.F.

Figure 279. Copper bell pendant. Western Mexico. Late Post-Classic Period, circa 1200–1550 A.D. Length 4 cm. (1⁹⁄₁₆ in.). Patina dark brown. Courtesy of the Museo Nacional de Antropología, Mexico, D.F.

278

279

Figure 280. Clay bell. Mexico. Late
Post-Classic Period, circa 1200–1550
A.D. Height 5 cm. (1¹⁵⁄₁₆ in.). Courtesy
of the Museo Nacional de Antropología,
Mexico, D.F.

Central America

Honduras Though many bells from Honduras have been recovered from the Sacred Well at Chichen Itza in Yucatan, Mexico, the cache which undoubtedly held the largest number of copper bells ever found in Honduras was the Quemislan Cave, located in the northwestern part of the country. Because at least several hundred copper bells were removed from the cave in the course of a number of excavations, it came to be called the "Quemislan Bell Cave." When discovered, it showed no signs of having been inhabited; there were no smoke-stained walls—the clearest clue to human use. It is 40 feet (12 meters) in width and 56 feet (17 meters) in depth. Its floor slopes at the uncomfortable angle of 45 degrees. The roof is 20 feet (6 meters) high at the cave's entrance, but its height decreases gradually until it is only 4 feet (1.2 meters) at the rear. The Quemislan Cave is located a short distance north of the Chamelecon River, about five miles (eight kilometers) from Naco, the site of an Aztec settlement, in the department of Santa Barbara.

It has been conjectured that either the bells once composed the stock of an itinerant Mexican trader and were hidden there or they were actually manufactured in the cave; beaten copper strips of irregular shape found inside the cave point to the latter theory.

Of much interest, because of their design as well as their imposing size, are the two copper bells shown in Figures 281 and 283. The one in Figure 281 depicts a turkey, its head turned backwards. The bell's suspension ring rests just below the bird's breast. One copper pellet is present. The copper bell in Figure 283 presents the well-defined features of the head of a rooster. This bell also contains a copper pellet.

The spherical copper bell depicted in Figure 282 displays the features of a monkey with eyebrows, eyes, nose, ears, and mouth standing out in bold relief. It is surmounted by a twofold round suspension ring resting upon a circular platform. No pellet is present.

281

282

Figure 281. Copper bell. Quemislan Cave, northwestern Honduras. Aztec Culture, circa 15th century A.D. Height 7.6 cm. (3 in.). Patina red. Courtesy of the Peabody Museum, Harvard University.

Figure 282. Copper bell. Honduras. Aztec Culture, circa 15th century A.D. Height 2.7 cm. (1¹⁄₁₆ in.). Patina light brown. Courtesy of the Peabody Museum, Harvard University.

Figure 283. Copper bell. Quemislan Cave, northwestern Honduras. Aztec Culture, circa 15th century A.D. Height 9.9 cm. (3⁷⁄₈ in.). Patina dark brown. Courtesy of the Peabody Museum, Harvard University.

Figure 284. Gold bell. Costa Rica. Circa 1200 A.D. Length 2.7 cm. (1 1/16 in.), weight 7.78 grams.

Figure 285. Gold bell. Costa Rica. Chiriquí Style, circa 1200 A.D. Height 2.8 cm. (1 1/8 in.), weight 11 grams. Courtesy of The Brooklyn Museum, Alfred W. Jenkins Fund.

284

285

Costa Rica According to a noted metallurgist, the late Professor William C. Root of Bowdoin College, the art of bell casting reached Costa Rica about 700 A.D. Bells have been found at numerous sites in the Linea Vieja area, in many instances along or near the banks of the Destierro, Revantazon, and Pacuare rivers. Graves in the Nicoya, San Carlos, and Diquis regions have yielded many bells of copper and gold as well as those in which gold or silver have been alloyed with copper as a base metal.

The only information available about the gold effigy bell in Plate 25 (p. 233) is that it is of Costa Rican provenance. It is an article of personal adornment and represents a war trophy, the severed head of an enemy. The bell was cast with a twofold suspension ring beneath its lower jaw and was worn upside down as a victor would carry home his trophy. That he did by attaching a light rope at the foramen magnum—the large opening at the base of the skull through which the spinal cord passes.

The gold bell in Figure 284 represents the head of a jaguar. Its lozenge-shaped eyes stand out in bold relief, as do also its snout and whiskers. The open mouth displays teeth irregularly set in both upper and lower jaws. Attached to the top of the head is an ovoid suspension loop. The bell contains a single gold pellet.

The gold ornament depicted in Plate 26 (pp. 234–235) is cast very realistically in the form of a spider. The arachnid's characteristic four pairs of legs are fully extended and joined at their extremities to an arch representing two twisted cords. The creature's abdomen is a spherical bell in which rolls a pellet.

The gold bell in Figure 285 is in the Chiriqui style. Resting upon a circular platform is a highly stylized form of a macaw with outstretched wings and upturned tail. The bell carries a single pellet.

Plate 25 (p. 233). Gold bell. Costa Rica.
Circa 1200 A.D. Height 3 cm. (1³⁄₁₆ in.),
weight 12.4 grams. Courtesy of The
Brooklyn Museum.

Plate 26 (pp. 234–235). Gold bell. Costa
Rica. Circa 1200 A.D. Length 9.5 cm.
(3¾ in.), width 8 cm. (3⅛ in.), weight
138.7 grams. Courtesy of The Brooklyn Museum.

*Plates 27 and 28 (p. 236). Gold bell.
Panama. Chiriquí Style, circa 12th
century A.D. Height 3.8 cm. (1½ in.),
weight 35.84 grams.*

*Plate 29 (p. 238). Gold bell. Panama.
Coclé Style, circa 12th century A.D.
Height 8 cm. (3⅛ in.), weight 37.5
grams. © National Geographic Society,
Washington, D.C.*

*Plate 30 (p. 239). Gold bell. Panama.
Coclé Style, circa 12th century A.D.
Height 8 cm. (3⅛ in.), weight 35
grams. © National Geographic Society, Washington, D.C.*

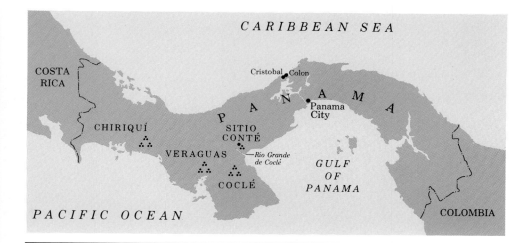

Panama

Bells which the Indians of Panama cast by the customary lost-wax method served chiefly as articles of personal adornment, though many were used in trade. They have been excavated in considerable quantities throughout the three provinces of Cocle, Veraguas, and Chiriqui. Such bells are of gold, copper, and *tumbaga*, the last-named a mixture of gold and copper in which silver frequently was present as an impurity. Spanish accounts referred to it as a low-grade gold. Numerous bells were gilded, and many were fashioned by the *mise en couleur* method. (See the descriptions of *tumbaga* and the *mise en couleur* method in the chapter on Mexico.)

The gold bell in Figure 286 dates from about 1400 A.D. It was found at Sitio Conte in Cocle Province on level land measuring some four or five acres and owned by a family named Conte. The site lies on the east bank of the Rio Grande de Cocle. Many bells of the same type have been found in other parts of Cocle Province. The body of the bell, which contains a gold pellet, is decorated with chevrons. Its tubular handle, composed of a series of rings and spirals, provides space for the insertion of a stick.

The gold bell portrayed in Figure 287 was excavated at Sitio Conte by the Harvard University Peabody Museum Expedition of 1933 under the direction of Dr. Samuel K. Lothrop (1892–1965). It came from Grave 1, Trench 1, where it lay with Skeleton II, an adult male. In an account of the excavation of that skeleton, Dr. Lothrop drew attention to the presence in its grave of objects of feminine use, such as nose rings of the type usually worn by women. He points out that the possibility must be entertained that Skeleton II represents a homosexual slave called a *camayoa*. Such slaves wore female attire and performed the household tasks traditionally relegated to women. Also found with the skeleton was a *metate*, a stone utensil used by Indian women to grind maize. The body of the bell is decorated with scrollwork. Like the bell in Figure 286, it also has a tubular handle for the insertion of a stick. Included in its midsection is the figure of a bird. No pellet is present.

The gold bell portrayed in Plates 27 and 28 (p. 236) represents a feline head with stylized ears in the form of crocodile heads in profile, crowned with spirals. An unusual feature is the feline's perforated eyes. Within its mouth rolls a stone pellet. The

Plate 31 (p. 240). Gold bell. Panama. Coclé Style, circa 12th century A.D. Height 7.5 cm. (2¹⁵⁄₁₆ in.), weight 21.5 grams. © National Geographic Society, Washington, D.C.

Figure 286. Gold bell. Coclé Province, Panama. Circa 12th century A.D. Height 5.2 cm. (2¹⁄₁₆ in.), weight 36.8 grams. Courtesy of the Peabody Museum, Harvard University.

Figure 287. Gold bell. Coclé Province, Panama. Circa 12th century A.D. Height 5.4 cm. (2⅛ in.), weight 33.5 grams. Courtesy of the Peabody Museum, Harvard University.

286

287

Figure 288. Copper bell. Panama. Circa 1200 A.D. Length 3.2 cm. (1¼ in.). Patina dark green.

Figure 290. Gold bell. Panama. Veraguas Style, circa 12th century A.D. Height 3.5 cm. (1⅜ in.), weight 28.77 grams.

Figure 289. Gold bead with bells. Veraguas Province, Panama. Circa 12th century A.D. Length 3.2 cm. (1¼ in.), weight 15.1 grams. Courtesy of the Peabody Museum, Harvard University.

288   290

presence of a suspension loop, cast with the bell, indicates that the object was worn as a pendant. The bell may be attributed to the Chiriqui culture.

Plates 29 (p. 238), 30 (p. 239), and 31 (p. 240) depict gold bells from the collection of the late Ferdinand Grebien. They may be attributed to the Cocle culture. The bodies of the bells are surmounted by platforms supporting, respectively, the recumbent forms of a jaguar, toucan, and armadillo. Each bell has a circular suspension ring and contains a gold pellet.

The gold pear-shaped Veraguas-style bell in Figure 290 dates from about the 12th century A.D. Its surface is smooth and undecorated except for a fine line which runs around the platform. The bell carries a round suspension ring cast as part of the bell. A small gold pellet is present.

The tubular gold bead portrayed in Figure 289 was identified by Dr. Lothrop and Dr. A. M. Tozzer as belonging to the Veraguas culture. It dates from about the 12th century A.D. and was acquired in 1939 from a local inhabitant of Ancon, Canal Zone. Cast with the bead are two gold bells, each containing a gold pellet. A number of such beads were often strung in necklaces.

289

The copper bell in Figure 288 is often called a "puzzle bell." Three views of it are depicted. The top view shows the full-faced features of the severed head of a slain enemy. The center one presents in profile a human head with a large nose. The bottom view portrays in profile an open-mouthed fish with a large dorsal fin. Like the gold effigy bell from Costa Rica pictured in Plate 25, this bell has a suspension ring under the jaw which enables it to be worn upside down as a pendant in the same way that a war trophy was customarily carried. The pellet is missing.

South America

Colombia

It is believed that the Indian tribes of Colombia gained their first knowledge of metallurgy and began making various objects of gold at the end of the first millennium B.C. Living in separate localities, the tribes developed their own cultures, and the pieces produced by their craftsmen possessed distinctive styles. Included among the objects of personal adornment were bells, earplugs, earrings, nose rings, and nose rods, as well as lip plugs, armbands, pectorals, penis covers, necklaces, and funerary masks.

Though the country was regarded as rich in gold, the Spaniards did not find there the amounts which they had expected. Other lands of the New World were later to provide far greater wealth for the Spanish Court.

In the 16th century, stories were recorded of the discovery of enormous gold bells, marking the location of Indian burial mounds. If such was the case, they were undoubtedly destroyed, for no such treasures exist today. For a period of 400 years after the conquest of Nueva Granada, now called Colombia, practically every gold object that fell into the hands of the invaders was melted down into bullion. This was generally done on American shores before it was shipped abroad to fill the coffers of foreign courts or to be placed on the world's gold market. Official records indicate that during the first 150 years after the Spaniards found gold in the Western Hemisphere, they shipped to the Old World 181 tons of the precious metal. Fortunately, most bells discovered in Colombia during the 19th century and later have been carefully preserved.

The Tairona Region

At the base of the northern and western slopes of the Sierra Nevada mountains of northern Colombia in the Magdalena Department, the Spanish conquistadors found the Tairona tribe. The skilled metallurgists of the Taironas produced many gold objects of personal adornment, including many elaborate nose ornaments, breast ornaments, small pendants, and necklaces. They also created gold bells of various shapes. Some were effigy bells.

The gold effigy bell from Minca depicted in Plate 32 (p. 249 left) shows a figure which has characteristics both anthropomorphic and zoomorphic. It carries an elaborate feathered headdress, studded with ornaments, generally found on both anthropomorphic and zoomorphic effigy bells. Just behind the headdress at the right and left are two suspension rings. Earrings are present and a lip plug appears just below the lower lip. A wide mouth displays the canine teeth of a jaguar. The human arms, adorned with armbands and bracelets, rest at the figure's sides, and the palms of the hands, with fingers extended, lie upon the abdomen—actually the bell's body. A gold pellet is present.

The gold bell from Minca in Plate 34 (p. 249 right) presents an anthropomorphic figure crowned by a feathered headdress. The lower lids of its beady eyes are sharply outlined, and there is a plug below the lower lip of its closed wide mouth. However, no arms or hands are present. Like the bell in Plate 32, it has two suspension rings and holds a gold pellet.

The gold bell from San Pedro de la Sierra, portrayed in Plate 33 (p. 249 center) likewise wears a headdress of feathers. A fierce expression is created by menacing jaguar fangs. This bell probably depicts a man wearing a jaguar mask to attribute to him that animal's savage qualities. Effigy bells possessing anthropomorphic and zoomorphic features are quite common in the Tairona area.

It is unusual to find in the Americas a bell of barrel-shaped form, such as the anthropomorphic effigy bell from Minca shown in Plate 35 (p. 250 left). On the bell's flat circular top are two multi-looped suspension rings, and equally spaced around its rim are four minute protuberances. These are apparently remnants of metal left in the channels (sprues) after the molten gold was poured into them during the casting process. No clapper is present, but there are two small holes in the bell's top for hanging one. Above the effigy's beady eyes are gracefully arched double eyebrows. A lower lip plug is present. Diminutive arms and hands rest alongside the body. A slit runs halfway up the mantle, on one side of which is welded a fin-shaped flange. A slight break in the line of joining is visible.

The ovoid bell from Bonda depicted in Plate 36 (p. 250 right) has anthropomorphic features characterized by minute bead-like eyes set far apart and a small nose formed by a double loop, under which rests an elongated mouth. Two suspension rings are cast on each side of the bell's flat top.

In Plate 37 (p. 251 left) is a Tairona necklace found at Minca. It is composed of twenty-six small gold bells in the form of frogs. A few of these contain tiny gold pellets. The bells are separated from one another by groups of spherical and tubular carnelian beads.

The Sinù Region In northwestern Colombia, directly south of the coastline marked by the Gulf of Uraba and the Caribbean, lie the fertile valleys of the Sinù, San Jorge, and Nechi rivers. Between the latter two flow the northern stretches of the Cauca. As the Spaniards invaded the land, looting its magnificent temples and many mound-shaped tombs, they found much gold. The few gold possessions of the Sinù Indians which did not fall into the hands of the Spanish plunderers and which are now in museums and private collections represent some of the finest examples of the Colombian metallurgist's art. Among the treasures are goblets, nose ornaments of the heavy, semicircular-ring type, fan-shaped ear ornaments cast in false filigree work, pendants in the form of flying fish, conical penis covers, and necklaces.

An example of a Sinù necklace is shown in Plate 38 (p. 251 right). It is composed of eight gold tubular beads and six gold bells. Three of the bells contain pellets, and these are also of gold. The upper sections of the bells' handles bear false filigree work. The necklace is not as long as the usual Indian necklace; perhaps some sections are missing.

The Quimbaya Region In the valleys midway down the Cauca and Magdalena rivers, in what is now the department of Quindío, lived the Quimbaya Indians. Among the abundant furnishings found in their tombs were quantities of unusual pottery, such as double vessels of zoomorphic form as well as those in the shape of human figures. Many pieces were decorated with intricately incised designs, and many were painted. The Quimbayas were rich in gold, as evidenced by the many gold objects unearthed throughout their territory, such as large lime containers, called *porporos*, some in the form of seated human figures and others presenting, in part, anthropomorphic features; and exquisitely modeled pendants in the form of stylized human figures and various animals, such as lizards and insects.

In comparison with the number of other gold objects found,

Plate 32° (p. 249 left). Gold bell. Minca, Magdalena Department, Colombia. Tairona Culture, circa 100 B.C.–1500 A.D. Height 3.2 cm. (1¼ in.), width 2.9 cm. (1⅛ in.), weight 13.5 grams. Courtesy of El Museo del Oro, Banco de la República, Bogotá.

Plate 33 (p. 249 center). Gold bell. San Pedro de la Sierra, Magdalena Department, Colombia, Tairona Culture, circa 100 B.C.–1500 A.D. Height 4.4 cm. (1¾ in.), width 3 cm. (1⅜ in.), weight 14.75 grams. Courtesy of El Museo del Oro, Banco de la República, Bogotá.

Plate 34 (p. 249 right). Gold bell. Minca, Magdalena Department, Colombia. Tairona Culture, circa 100 B.C.–1500 A.D. Height 2.7 cm. (1⅛ in.), width 2.3 cm. (⅞ in.), weight 6.95 grams. Courtesy of El Museo del Oro, Banco de la República, Bogotá.

Plate 35 (p. 250 left). Gold bell. Minca. Magdalena Department, Colombia. Tairona Culture, circa 100 B.C.–1500 A.D. Height 5.2 cm. (2 1/16 in.), width 4.1 cm. (1 5/8 in.), weight 36.2 grams. Courtesy of El Museo del Oro, Banco de la República, Bogotá.

Plate 36 (p. 250 right). Gold bell. Bonda, Magdalena Department, Colombia. Tairona Culture, circa 100 B.C.–1500 A.D. Height 3.4 cm. (1 3/8 in.), width 3.2 cm. (1 1/4 in.), weight 11.45 grams. Courtesy of El Museo del Oro, Banca de la República, Bogotá.

Plate 37 (p. 251 left). Necklace with gold bells (frogs) and carnelian beads. Minca, Magdalena Department, Colombia. Tairona Culture, circa 100 B.C.– 1500 A.D. Length of necklace 87 cm. (34¼ in.). Courtesy of El Museo del Oro, Banco de la República, Bogotá.

Plate 38 (p. 251 right). Necklace with gold bells and gold beads. Sinú, Córdoba Department, Colombia. Sinú Style, circa 100 B.C.–1500 A.D. Length of necklace 41.3 cm. (16¼ in.). Beads: length 4.5 cm. (1¾ in.), diameter 0.8 cm. (⁵⁄₁₆ in.), total weight 184.4 grams. Courtesy of El Museo del Oro, Banco de la República, Bogotá.

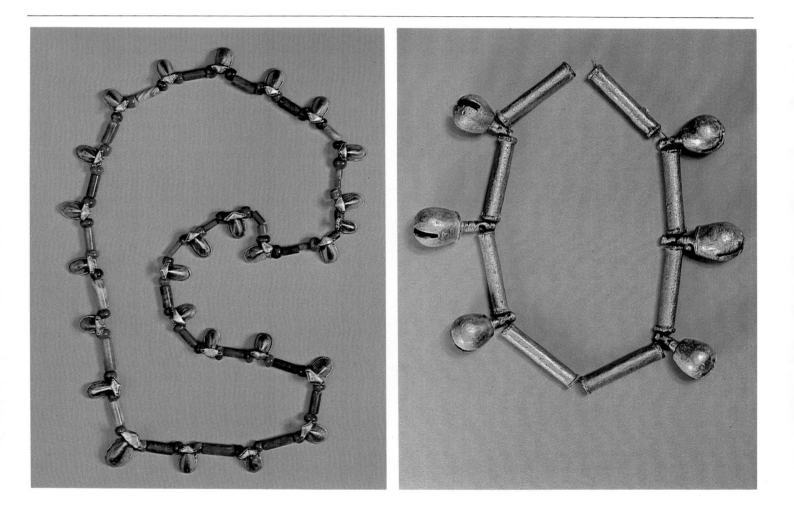

Plate 39 (p. 252 left). Gold bell. Quindío Department, Colombia. Quimbaya Style, circa 100 B.C.–1500 A.D. Height 3.3 cm. (1¼ in.) diameter 1.5 cm. (⅝ in.), weight 14.75 grams. Courtesy of El Museo del Oro, Banco de la República. Bogotá.

Plate 40 (p. 252 center). Gold bell. Quindío Department, Colombia. Quimbaya Style, circa 100 B.C.–1500 A.D. Height 3.3 cm. (1¼ in.), diameter 2.7 cm. (1¹⁄₁₆ in.), weight 17.9 grams. Courtesy of El Museo del Oro, Banco de la República, Bogotá.

Plate 41 (p. 252 right). Gold bell. Quindío Department, Colombia. Quimbaya Style, circa 100 B.C.–1500 A.D. Height 6.4 cm. (2½ in.), width 4 cm. (1⁹⁄₁₆ in.), weight 37.3 grams. Courtesy of El Museo del Oro, Banco de la República, Bogotá.

Plate 42 (p. 253 left). Gold bell. Quindío Department, Colombia. Quimbaya Style, circa 100 B.C.–1500 A.D. Height 4.2 cm. (1⅝ in.), diameter 1.5 cm. (⅝ in.), weight 14.8 grams. Courtesy of El Museo del Oro, Banco de la República, Bogotá.

Plate 43 (p. 253 right). Gold bell. Colombia. Quimbaya Style, circa 100 B.C.–1500 A.D. Height 2.2 cm. (1¼₁₆ in.), width 2.7 cm. (1¹⁄₁₆ in.), weight 13.9 grams. Courtesy of El Museo del Oro, Banco de la República, Bogotá.

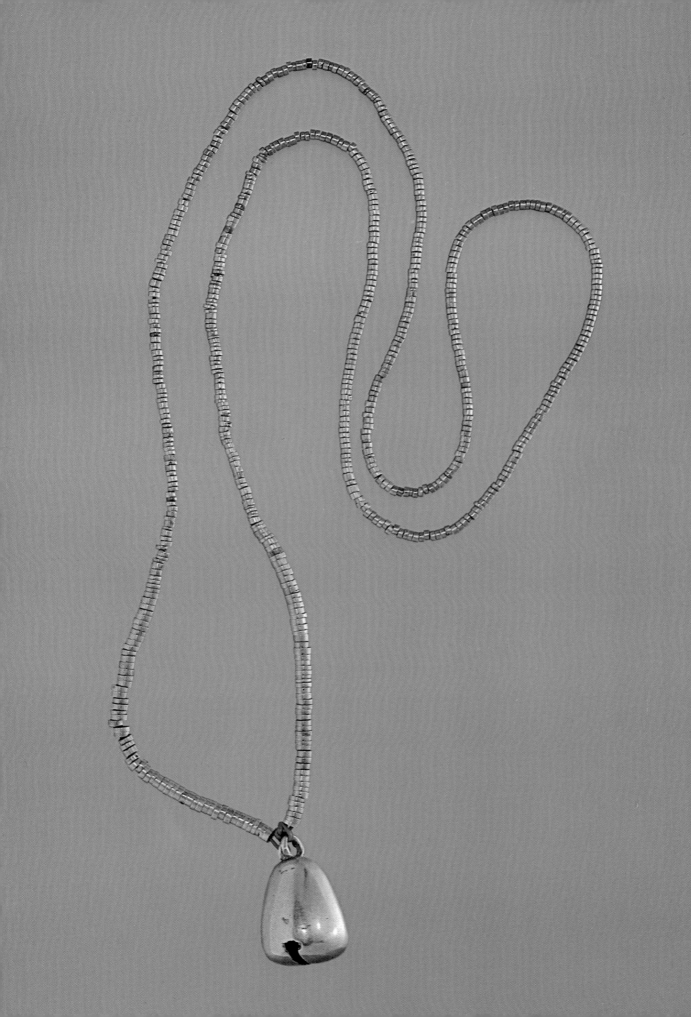

Plate 44 (p. 254). Gold bell. Colombia. Nariño Style, circa 100 B.C.-1500 A.D. Height 3.5 cm. (1⅜ in.). Necklace: 664 gold cylindrical beads. Length 105 cm. (41⁵⁄₁₆ in.), total weight 75 grams. Courtesy of The Brooklyn Museum.

Figure 291. Gold bell. Pupiales, Nariño Department, Colombia. Nariño Style, circa 100 B.C.–1500 A.D. Height 3.3 cm. (1⁵⁄₁₆ in.), width 4 cm. (1⁹⁄₁₆ in.), weight 47.4 grams. Courtesy of El Museo del Oro, Banco de la República, Bogotá.

bells have been few indeed. The gold bells in Plates 39–42 (pp. 252–253) were unearthed in the Quindio Department, territory lying within the Quimbaya archaeological region. They are well preserved. Each contains a single pellet. Plate 43 (p. 253 right) shows a gold bell of Quimbaya style. Its provenance is not known. The bell is topped by a semicircular suspension ring and holds a gold pellet.

The Nariño Region

In the Andean region of southwestern Colombia, just north of the Ecuadorian border, lived the Nariño Indians. A study of the characteristics of their pottery and myriad gold objects reveals a strong artistic influence from both Ecuador and Peru. Relatively few gold bells have been found in Narino graves in contrast to other gold objects of adornment. Prevalent have been nose rings, ear plugs, breastplates and circular plaques. Repousse work of geometric and stylized animal designs characterized many of the plaques that were sewed upon ceremonial and everyday garments. Most Nariño archaeological finds have been unearthed in the vicinity of the municipalities of Ipiales, Iles, Tuquerres, and Pupiales. It was in the last-named that the gold pear-shaped bell pictured in Figure 291 was found. The bell has a smooth, shiny surface. There are two holes in the top of the bell for suspending it. A metal pellet is present.

291

The necklace in Plate 44 (p. 254) is composed of 664 thin, cylindrical gold beads, graduated in size, and a pear-shaped gold bell of the Nariño style. The bell is surmounted by a circular suspension ring and contains a metal pellet.

Ecuador

It is believed that metallurgy was introduced into Ecuador from Peru during the 3rd century B.C. One of the richest archaeological sites, which yielded valuable finds for many years, was La Tolita in the northern part of Esmeraldas Province. The Tolita culture flourished several centuries before and after the Christian era. Its metallurgists were renowned for their production of fabulous objects of gold, copper, and tumbaga. Among them were a wide variety of small masks, rings, nose ornaments, pins, needles, fishhooks, beads, and bells.

Archaeological finds in the central and southern highlands of the country, though less spectacular, perhaps, than those from

Figure 292. Copper bells. Ecuador. Manteño Style, circa 850–1500 A.D. Average height 0.6 cm. (¼ in.). 101 copper bells arranged as a necklace, length 62.2 cm. (24½ in.).

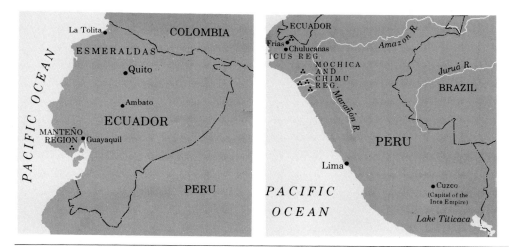

the coastal regions, have, nevertheless, contributed their share of information about the life and customs of Ecuador's early inhabitants.

Illustrated in Figure 292 is a necklace of the Manteño culture (circa 850–1500 A.D.). It has been assembled from 101 spherical copper bells excavated from a grave. The bells contain no pellets. An interesting feature is the presence of single minute, cylindrical seashell beads adhering to each of two bells near the upper part of the necklace—an indication that other such beads, probably overlooked at the time of excavation, may have been part of the original necklace.

Peru

Following the identical pattern set by their countrymen in the northern lands of South America, Meso-America, and Mexico, the merciless, gold-hungry conquistadors under Francisco Pizarro and Diego de Almagro collected all golden objects within their reach throughout the great Inca Empire of Peru and melted them down into bullion for shipment to Spain. There, it was promptly minted into coins to finance the imperial wars of Charles V.

In accumulating vast treasure from the Incas, the Spaniards failed, however, to obtain all of Peru's golden wealth. Huge quantities of buried gold objects used for ritual as well as ordinary purposes, discovered centuries later by both skilled archaeologists and *huaqueros* (grave robbers), have given many others the opportunity to see, admire, and sometimes acquire beautiful creations of Peruvian master craftsmen.

Among Peruvian finds dating from the initial knowledge of metallurgy in the Western Hemisphere have come down to us bells of gold, silver, bronze, copper, and *champi*, an alloy composed of about 95 percent copper, 4 percent silver, and 1 percent gold. The word *champi* is derived from Quechua, often called Incan, the native language of Peru during that period; it is still widely spoken in parts of Peru, Argentina, Bolivia, Chile, and Ecuador. Many Peruvian bells are in the shape of small cones made from beaten sheets of metal. Others have been cast.

Plate 45 (p. 260) portrays a necklace composed of 226 gold bells of graduated size. It was excavated from a tomb in the Vicus

Figure 293. Copper ornament with bells. Peru. Mochica Culture, 4th–5th century A.D. *Height 8.9 cm. (3½ in.), width 17.8 cm. (7 in.). Patina mottled light green and reddish brown.*

Plate 45 (p. 260). Necklace of gold bells. Vicus Region, Piura Province, Peru. Circa 200 B.C.–300 A.D. Length 113 cm. (44½ in.), height of largest bell 1.3 cm. (½ in.). Courtesy of Colección Mujica Gallo del Oro del Perú, Lima.

Plate 46 (p. 262). Gold breastplates. Frias, Piura Province, Peru. Mochica Culture, 2nd–4th century A.D. Left: length 26.5 cm. (10⁷⁄₁₆ in.), diameter of disk 9 cm. (3⁹⁄₁₆ in.). Right: length 18.5 cm. (7¼ in.), diameter of disk 9 cm. (3⁹⁄₁₆ in.). Courtesy of Colección Mujica Gallo del Oro del Perú, Lima.

Plate 47 (p. 263). Necklace with gold bells. Frias, Piura Province, Peru. Mochica Culture, 2nd–4th century A.D. Length 53.5 cm. (21¹⁄₁₆ in.), height of largest bell 3.2 cm. (1¼ in.). Courtesy of Colección Mujica Gallo del Oro del Perú, Lima.

region of Piura Province and may be dated from about 200 B.C. to 300 A.D. In addition to objects of high gold content, the metallurgists of the Vicus region made frequent use of gold plating on copper and the *mise en couleur* method.

Figure 293 shows a large crescent-shaped copper ornament which may have been worn at ceremonies. This object is of the Mochica culture 4th–5th century A.D. To create it the metallurgist first hammered out a thin sheet of copper; then, having placed it over a negative form carved out of stone or very hard wood, he hammered it into the desired shape, obtaining fourteen semicircular indentations. Two oval sections were then cut out near the center of the plate, and it was folded in half. Afterwards, a copper pellet was inserted in each of the seven bells thus formed. Sections of the object have been badly damaged by corrosion, and only two of the pellets remain.

In Plate 46 (p. 262) are two gold breastplates of the Mochica culture. These objects, which may be dated 2nd–4th century A.D., were found in a tomb near Frias, a village in the mountainous area of Piura Province and lying about twenty-five miles (forty kilometers) north of the town of Chulucanas. The breastplates are of high quality gold (over twenty carats). Each disk is ornamented with the applique of a jaguar's head, tongue extended. Hanging below the disk of each breastplate is a trapezoidal plate to which is attached a group of four conical bells without clappers; to make them ring they were swung and struck against one another. At each side hang thin gold ribbons, cut out to resemble moving serpents, their heads realistically hammered in relief. In the center of the breastplate at the left hangs a tongue-shaped appendage, decorated at the top with a zoomorphic repousse design. That at the right carries none.

Plate 49 (p. 265) depicts a Mochica necklace unearthed near Frias. It is composed of groups of minute beads cut from red seashells and ten gold conical bells which alternate with twelve silver head bells. With one exception, none of the gold bells contains a clapper, and clappers are also absent from the silver head bells. Just below the facial features of each silver head bell runs an openwork design of spirals. The central ornament of the necklace is a badly crushed gold miniature of a water jug with ovoid bottom.

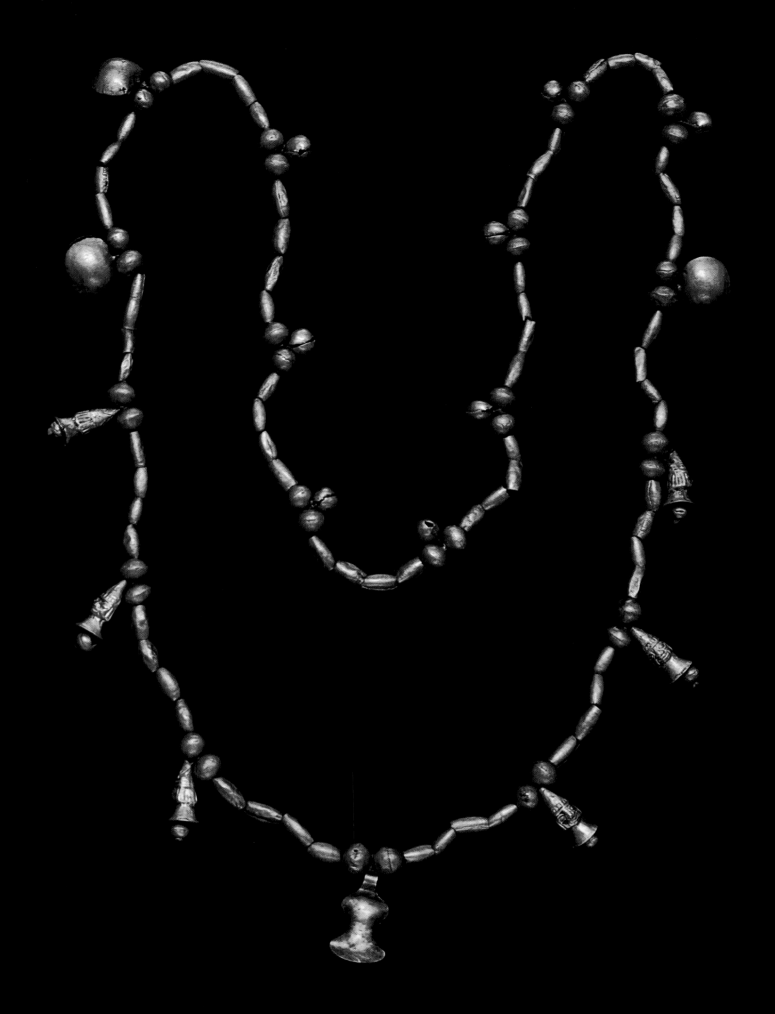

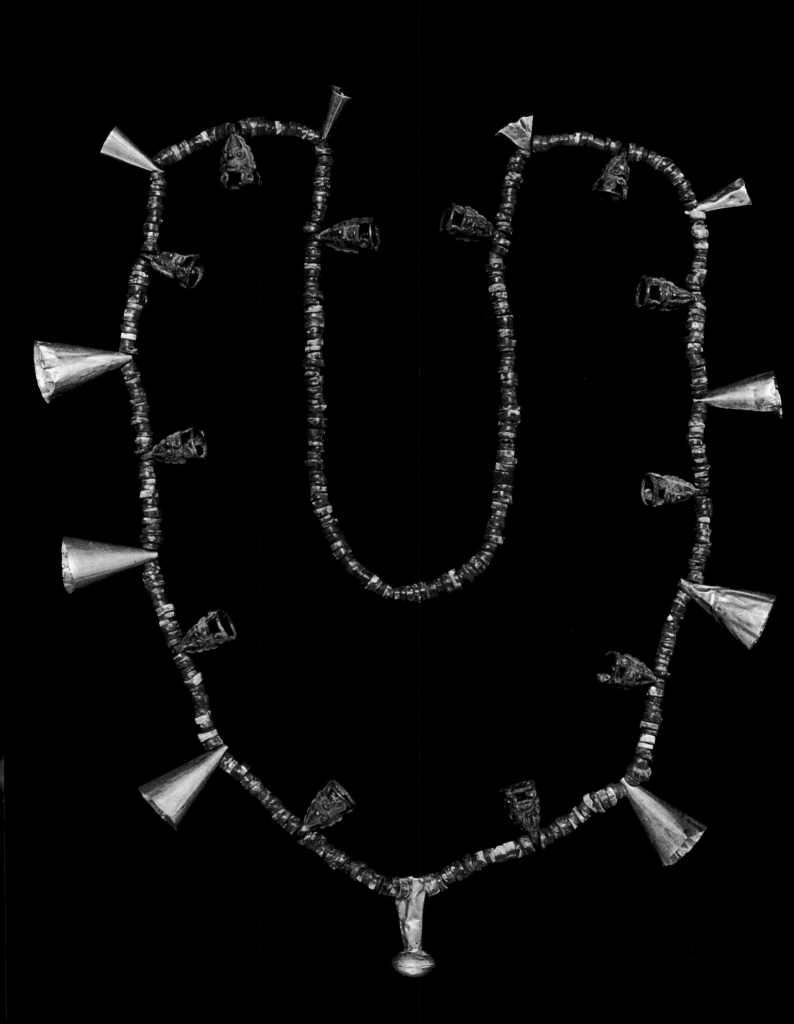

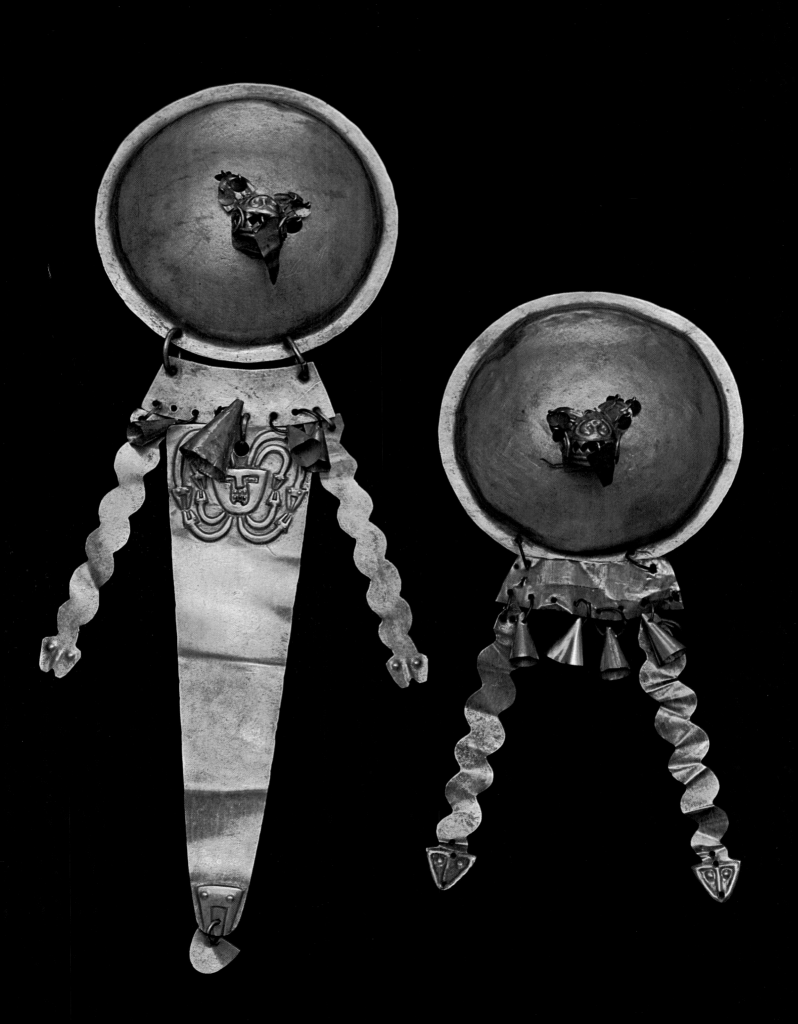

Plate 48 (p. 264) and Figure 294. Necklace with gold bells. Northern Peru. Chimu Culture, 11th–15th century A.D. Length 131.5 cm. (51¾ in.), height of each clam-shaped bell 2 cm. (¾ in.), height of each effigy bell 2.5 cm. (1 in.). Courtesy of Colección Mujica Gallo del Oro del Perú, Lima.

Plate 49 (p. 265). Necklace with gold and silver bells. Frias, Piura Province, Peru. Mochica Culture, circa 2nd–4th century A.D. Length of necklace 98.1 cm. (38⅝ in.), height of gold bell 3 cm. (1³⁄₁₆ in.), height of silver bell 2 cm. (²⁵⁄₃₂ in.). Courtesy of Colección Mujica Gallo del Oro del Perú, Lima.

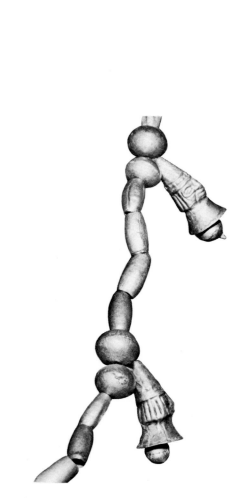

294

From another Mochica grave near Frias comes the necklace shown in Plate 47 (p. 263). It is composed of thirty-one gold conical bells strung between small lobed, flanged disks and plates. Below these hangs a thin strip of gold cut in the form of a serpent, a head at each end. Under it are three gold cones with solid bases and two small fan-shaped plates separated by a large flanged, semi-spherical bead. At the very bottom is suspended a gold tweezers in the shape of a half-moon supporting the forms of two serpents with heads at their ends. Male Peruvians of ancient times used tweezers to pull out all their facial hair.

Graves and ruins of cities along Peru's extensive coastline and river valleys, such as the Pacasmayo, Chicama, Moche, and Viru, have yielded many necklaces composed either entirely of bells or of bells combined with gold beads and various precious and semiprecious stones—emerald, topaz, amethyst, turquoise, lapis lazuli, jade, pink quartz, rock crystal, and malachite. Some necklaces contained pearls. Many bore gold idols inlaid with turquoise.

The necklace portrayed in Plate 48 (p. 264) a detail of which appears in Figure 294, may be dated from the 11th to the 15th century. It is Chimu, a culture of the coastal and river valley areas which reached its zenith from the 13th to the 14th century and was finally supplanted by that of the all-powerful Incas. The necklace is entirely of gold. Its central ornament is a tweezers suspended from lozenge-shaped and round beads arranged in groups to hold three clam-shaped crotal bells and six effigy bells with swinging clappers. Each clapper terminates in a spherical bead. Portrayed in effigy is Naym-Lap, legendary King of the Lambayeques and father of their culture. The king wears a pointed cap.

At an undetermined time between the 12th and 13th centuries A.D., the Lambayeques had been conquered by the Chimu, their lands annexed by the Chimu Empire, and their culture absorbed. A priest who accompanied Francisco Pizarro and his small band of followers when they landed in 1532 at Tumbes, near the Ecuadorian border, wrote that among the Indian prisoners was one who told him of an ancient legend, handed down from generation to generation, describing how, over a thousand years before, King Naym-Lap had come by boat to the coast of Lambayeque from a distant land somewhere in the Pacific.

Plate 50 (pp. 268–269). Silver bells. Peru. Chimu Culture, 11th–15th century A.D. Left: height 7 cm. (2¾ in.), width 3.5 cm. (1⅜ in.), depth 3.5 cm. (1⅜ in.). Right: height 7 cm. (2¾ in.), width 4 cm. (1⁹⁄₁₆ in.), depth 4 cm. (1⁹⁄₁₆ in.). Courtesy of Colección Mujica Gallo del Oro del Perú, Lima.

Plate 51 (pp. 270–271). Copper bells. Peru. Mochica Culture, 4th–5th century A.D. Left: height 3.8 cm. (1½ in.), width 3.7 cm. (1⁷⁄₁₆ in.). Patina light green. Right: height 3.8 cm. (1½ in.), width 3.5 cm. (1⅜ in.). Patina light green.

Figure 295. Bronze staff head with bells. Peru. Chimu Culture, 11th–15th century A.D. Height 10.8 cm. (4¼ in.). Patina dark brown. Courtesy of the John D. Green Collection.

The Chimu bronze staff head in Figure 295 is in the form of a bowl with four young birds, wings outspread, perched around its rim. Attached near the bottom of the bowl, open for the insertion of a staff, are four loops, each holding a bell containing a pellet.

In Plate 50 (pp. 268–269) are two Chimu tetragonal silver bells. Their sides flare from the rounded edges of flat crowns. Each bell has two holes in its top through which cords were passed to attach the bells to a dancer's garment.

Two clam-shaped copper bells of the Mochica culture are portrayed in Plate 51 (pp. 270–271). They may be dated between the 4th and the 5th century A.D. These bells were created in the same manner as the copper ornament depicted in Figure 293. On one side of each bell a human face stands out in bold relief. The surface of the other side is plain. Each bell has a single hole at the top so that, like those in Plate 50, it could be fastened to a garment. Only the bell at the left has retained its pellet which is a pebble.

Dr. Junius Bird, Curator Emeritus of Anthropology of the American Museum of Natural History, has pointed out to this author that the limited use of the *cire perdue* method in Peru in the casting of bells may be explained by the fact that there were no colonies of wax-producing bees either in the highlands or coastal regions of Peru. Dr. Bird observed that records show that during their occupation of Peru, the Spaniards learned that one tribe of Indians in the western Amazon Basin had been supplying the inhabitants of the highlands with limited amounts of wax. In order to obtain wax for church candles, the Spaniards imposed a tax to be paid in wax by the Indians. He said that records also show that those Indians sent a delegation to Peru to protest that they were unable to meet the quota demanded by the Spaniards.

Between the 13th and middle of the 15th century A.D., the Incas, who had originated as a small tribe in the Cuzco Valley of Peru, had formed a powerful empire, which included large parts of what is present-day Peru, Ecuador, Bolivia, Chile, and an area of northwestern Argentina. When the Spaniards arrived, the Inca Empire was at the height of its glory but after the death of its ruler, Huayna Capac, it had been weakened by a struggle for

295

Figures 296–297. *Bronze bell (obverse and reverse views). Cuzco, Peru. Late Inca Period, 16th century* A.D. *Height 5.2 cm.* (2¹⁄₁₆ *in.), diameter 4 cm.* (1⁹⁄₁₆ *in.). Patina dark green. Courtesy of the Miriam Colvin Truesdell Collection.*

Figures 298–299. *Champi bells. Cuzco, Peru. Late Inca Period, 16th century* A.D. *298: height 5.7 cm.* (2¼ *in.), diameter 4.4 cm.* (1¾ *in.). Patina gray. 299: height 5 cm.* (1¹⁵⁄₁₆ *in.), diameter 1.6 cm.* (⅝ *in.). Patina light green.*

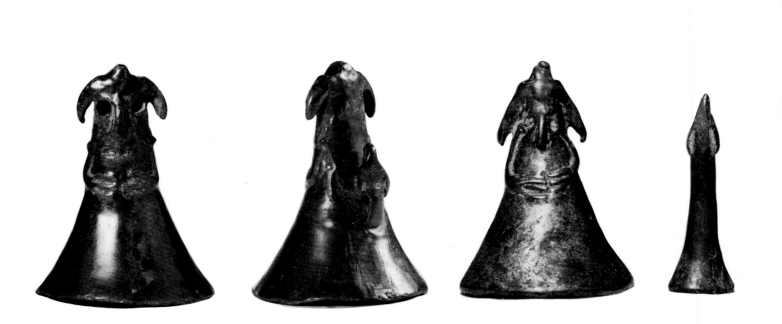

296-299

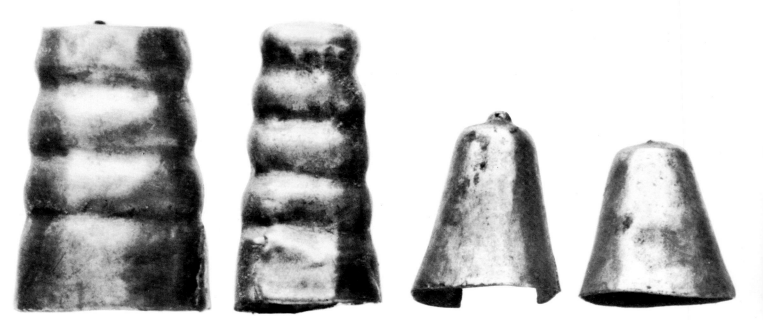

300-303

Figures 300–301. Gold bells. Compañia Baja, Coquimbo Province, Chile. Diaguita Culture, 15th–16th century A.D. *300: height 1.6 (⅝ in.), diameter 1.1 cm. (⁷⁄₁₆ in.). 301: height 1.6 cm. (⅝ in.), diameter 0.8 cm. (⁵⁄₁₆ in.). Courtesy of the Museum of the American Indian, New York.*

Figures 302–303. Gold bells. Compañia Baja, Coquimbo Province, Chile. Diaguita Culture, 15th–16th century A.D. *302: height 1.3 cm. (½ in.), diameter 0.8 cm. (⁵⁄₁₆ in.). 303: height 1.1 cm. (⁷⁄₁₆ in.), diameter 1 cm. (⅜ in.). Courtesy of the Museum of the American Indian, New York.*

the crown between his sons, Huascar and Atahualpa. In the conflict, Atahualpa had emerged victorious. During that period of dissension, Pizarro, with minimal opposition and a reported force of but 62 cavalrymen and 106 foot soldiers, marched into the mountains to Cajamarca, where he guilefully ambushed and captured Atahualpa. Then, after having received a ransom for his release, Pizarro had him executed by garroting.

Figures 296–297 show two views of a bronze effigy bell belonging to the Late Inca Period. The front view presents a stylized, diminutive human figure, its hands resting upon its abdomen in a position similar to the hands on the Tairona gold effigy bell in Plate 32. Its eyes are represented by holes. The rear view reveals a small bird clinging to the back of the bell's mantle. At the top are two holes for suspending the bell. No clapper is present.

The *champi* bells in Figures 298–299 are without clappers. Both bells resemble, in varying degrees, the bell in Figures 296–297. These bells were obtained by the author in Cuzco and, like the one in Figures 296–297, have been identified as of the Late Inca Period. Bells of the form described have appeared from time to time in the markets of La Paz, Bolivia.

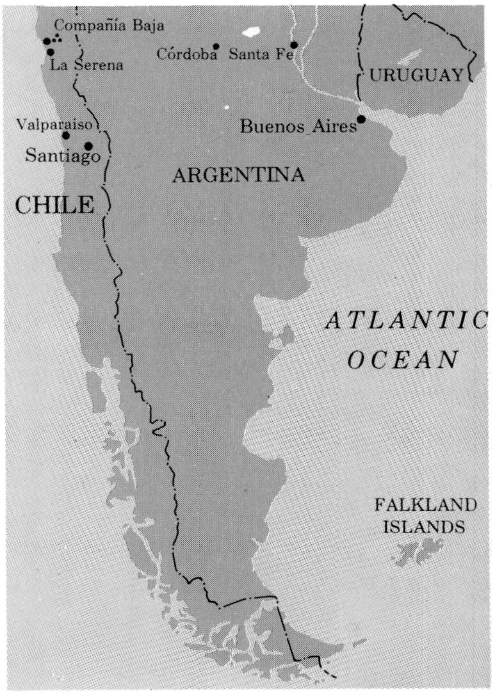

In Figures 300–301 are two bells of hammered gold which were found about 1939 by Dr. Samuel K. Lothrop while he was heading the Mrs. Thea Heye–Lothrop Expedition. The digging took place at La Serena, Coquimbo Province, and in the surrounding area of the Chilean coast. The actual excavation site was Compañia Baja. The bells were made by the Diaguita Indians, whose culture flourished in Chile during the 15th and 16th centuries A.D. and spread over the northwestern portion of modern-day Argentina into the mountainous provinces of Salta, Tucuman, Catamarca, La Rioja, and San Juan. The bells are cylindrical with horizontally corrugated surfaces. Atop each is a small hole through which originally passed a string to attach the bell to a dancer's garment. These bells, undoubtedly grouped with others, were not intended to hold swinging clappers; instead, their sounds were produced as they struck one another during a dance. In Figures 302–303 are two cup-shaped bells; the one in Figure 302 is slightly damaged. They too were excavated at Compañia

Chile

Figure 304. Bronze bell. La Palla, Cachí, Salta Province, Argentina. Culture unknown, circa 15th century A.D. Height 19.2 cm. (7⁹⁄₁₆ in.), diameter 20.3 cm. (8 in.), depth 7.1 cm. (2¹³⁄₁₆ in.). Patina traces of light green. Courtesy of the Museum für Völkerkunde, Berlin.

Figure 305. Bronze bell. Curtiembre, Entre Ríos Province, Argentina. Culture unknown, circa 15th century A.D. Height 20.2 cm. (7¹⁵⁄₁₆ in.), diameter 19 cm. (7½ in.), depth 8.2 cm. (3¼ in.). Patina light green. Courtesy of the Museum für Völkerkunde, Berlin.

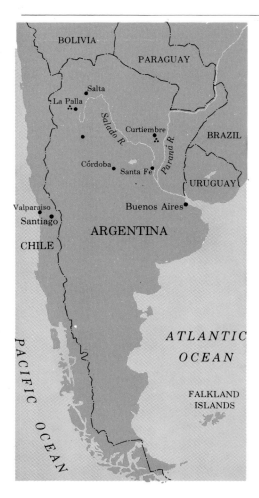

Baja. A 1940 analysis of their composition by the late Professor William C. Root indicated a content of 80 percent gold and 20 percent silver. The single holes punched in the bells' crowns served the same purpose as those in the bells shown in Figures 300–301.

The bronze bells appearing in Figures 304 and 305 date from the 15th century A.D. They were found in northwestern and east central Argentina, respectively. However, it is not known by what tribe or tribes they were cast. The bell in Figure 304 was found at La Palla, Cachí, in the province of Salta. It is of elliptical shape. On the flat oval top are three sprue marks. Three metal bars previously stood upright there, having been formed when molten metal was poured into the runners or pouring ducts (sprues) to fill the mold. The metal bars later were lopped off. There is a slight outward flare to the bell's mouth around which, in low relief, runs a single narrow line. This supports a pair of human figures readily distinguishable when the bell is turned upside down. The faces have almost circular eyes and elliptical mouths. Groups of triangles form the bodies. The clapper is missing.

Also of elliptical shape is the bell in Figure 305, found at Curtiembre, in the province of Entre Rios. In this bell's flat top are two round holes for the suspension of a round clapper, found with the bell. Atop the bell are two sprue marks, the one on the left quite distinct, the other barely visible. Running in relief above the bell's mouth is a band of geometric design supporting identical single human figures, which appear in sharp relief on each side of the bell. They are clearly observable when the bell is inverted. Their eyes are triangular, and their straight mouths display teeth. The bells were undoubtedly worn by llamas; it was the custom to place a bell at the neck of the male llama leading the herd. At times, a bell was worn by an old female llama that had borne no offspring but had been selected as a leader.

304

305

Bibliography Addison, Frank. *The Wellcome Excavations in the Sudan.* Oxford University Press, London, 1949.

Alexander, John. *Jugoslavia Before the Roman Conquest.* Thames and Hudson, Ltd., London, 1972.

Bakay, Kornél. *Scythian Rattles in the Carpathian Basin and Their Eastern Connections.* Akadémiai Kiadó, Budapest, 1971.

Baumann, Hans. *The Land of Ur.* Oxford University Press, London, 1969.

Bequignon, Yves. *Recherches Archeologiques à Phères de Thessalie.* Les Belles Lettres, Paris, 1937.

Bunker, Emma C., Chatwin, C. Bruce, and Farkas, Ann R. *"Animal Style" Art from East to West.* The Asia Society, New York, 1970.

Burland, C. A. (An Introduction and Notes on the Plates.) *Magic Books from Mexico.* Ediciones Lara, Mexico, 1966.

Ceram, C. W. *Gods, Graves, and Scholars.* Alfred A. Knopf, Inc., New York, 1951.

Christensen, Arthur. *L'Iran sous les Sassanides.* P. Geuthner, Paris, 1936.

Dawson, Raymond. *The Legacy of China.* The University Press, Oxford, 1964.

Delougaz, Pinhas, and Haines, Richard C. *A Byzantine Church at Khirbat Al-Karak.* University of Chicago Oriental Institute, Chicago, 1960.

Desmond, Alice Curtis. *Cleopatra's Children.* Dodd, Mead & Company, New York, 1971.

Egami, Namio. *The Beginnings of Japanese Art.* Weatherhill, New York, and Heibonsha, Tokyo, 1973.

Frye, Richard N. *The Heritage of Persia.* Weidenfeld and Nicolson, London, 1962.

Ghirshman, R. *Iran.* Penguin Books, Baltimore, 1954.

Grenier, Albert. *Bologne, Villanovienne et Etrusque VIIIᵉ–IVᵉ Siècles avant Notre Ere.* Fontemoing et Cie., Paris, 1912.

Heurgon, Jacques. *Daily Life of the Etruscans.* The Macmillan Company, New York, 1964.

Howorth, H. H. "The Avars." *Journal of the Royal Asiatic Society,* New Series, Vol. XXI, London, 1889.

Josephus, Flavius. *The Jewish War,* revised, Vol. II. American Book Exchange, New York, 1880.

Karlbeck, Orvar. *Treasure Seeker in China.* The Cresset Press, London, 1957.

King, Blanche Busey. *Under Your Feet.* Dodd, Mead & Company, New York, 1948.

Laszlo, Gyula. *Etudes Archeologiques sur l'Histoire de la Societe des Avars.* Budapest, 1955.

Layard, Austen Henry. *Nineveh and Its Remains.* 2 volumes; G. P. Putnam & Co., New York, 1852.

Legrain, Leon. *Luristan Bronzes in the University Museum.* University of Pennsylvania, Philadelphia, 1934.

Lothrop, Samuel Kirkland. "Metals from the Cenote of Sacrifice, Chichen Itza, Yucatan." *Memoirs of the Peabody Museum of Archaeology and Ethnology, Harvard University,* Vol. X, No. 2, Cambridge, Mass., 1952.

———. "Cocle: An Archaeological Study of Central Panama." *Memoirs of the Peabody Museum of Archaeology and Ethnology, Harvard University*, Vols. VII and VIII, Cambridge, Mass., 1937–42.

MacKendrick, Paul. *The Iberian Stones Speak*. Funk & Wagnalls, New York, 1969.

Mallowan, Max E. L. *Nimrud and Its Remains*. William Collins Sons & Co., Ltd., London, 1966.

Mayer, Josephine, and Prideaux, Tom. *Never to Die*. The Viking Press, New York, 1938.

Morgan, Jacques Jean Marie de. *Mission Scientifique en Perse*, Tome IV. Ernest Leroux, Editeur, Paris, 1896.

Munroe, Henry S. "Prehistoric Bronze Bells from Japan." *Annals of the New York Academy of Sciences*, Vol. I, No. 2, New York, 1877.

Phillips, E. D. *The Royal Hordes: Nomad Peoples of the Steppes*. Thames and Hudson, Ltd., London, 1965.

Phillips, Wendell. *Qataban and Sheba*. Victor Gollancz, Ltd., London, 1955.

Pike, Donald G., and Muench, David. *Anasazi: Ancient People of the Rock*. American West Publishing Company, Palo Alto, Calif., 1974.

Piotrovskii, B. B. *Urartu*. Frederick A. Praeger, New York, 1967.

Posener, Georges. *Dictionary of Egyptian Civilization*. Tudor Publishing Company, New York, 1959.

Randall-MacIver, David. *Villanovans and Early Etruscans*. Clarendon Press, Oxford, 1924.

Rawlinson, George (trans.). *The History of Herodotus*, Vols. I and II. J. M. Dent & Sons, Ltd., Toronto, and E. P. Dutton & Co., Inc., New York, 1910.

Roux, Georges. *Ancient Iraq*. Penguin Books Ltd., Harmondsworth, Eng., 1966.

Shaw, Thurstan. *Igbo-Ukwu*, Vols. I and II. Northwestern University Press, Evanston, Ill., 1970.

Steward, Julian H. "The Andean Civilizations." In *Handbook of South American Indians*, Vol. II. U.S. Government Printing Office, Washington, D.C., 1946.

Stone, Doris, and Balser, Carlos. *Aboriginal Metalwork in Lower Central America*. San Jose, Costa Rica, 1967.

Sulimirski, T. *The Sarmatians*. Thames and Hudson, Ltd., London, 1970.

Vaillant, George C. *Aztecs of Mexico*, revised. Doubleday & Company, Inc., Garden City, N.Y., 1962.

Watson, William. *Archaeology in China*. Max Parrish & Co. Ltd., London, 1960.

———. *China*. Frederick A. Praeger, New York, 1961.

Willey, Gordon R. *An Introduction to American Archaeology*. Prentice-Hall, Inc., Englewood Cliffs, N.J., 1966–71.

Wylie, A. *Notes on Chinese Literature*. The American Presbyterian Press, Shanghai, 1902.

Index Numbers in italics indicate illustrations.

Illustration Credits

Louis F. Barriga G., Plates 32, 33, 34, 35, 36, 37, 38, 39, 40, 41, 42, 43

Lee Boltin, Figure 148; Plates 1, 2, 3, 4, 9, 10 and 11, 12, 13, 14, 15, 16, 17, 22, 23, 51

Victor R. Boswell, Jr., Plates 29, 30, 31

Paul Brenner, Figures 18, 19, 258–261

Hillel Burger, Plates 18, 19, 20, 21

Bart J. DeVito, Plates 27 and 28; Jacket illustrations

Ramón Enriquez R., Figures 270, 271, 272

Carmelo Guadagno, Figures 300–301, 302–303

Helga Photo Studio, Inc., Figures 29, 33, 36, 44, 45, 48, 49, 74 and 75, 121 and 122, 147, 160–162, 189, 251, 252, 263, 264, 265, 269, 284, 288, 291, 292, 293, 295, 296–297

William Lyall, Plates 25, 26, 44

O. E. Nelson, Figures 90, 150

Jorge Neumann, Plates 45, 46, 47, 48, 49, 50

Raoul Sallis, Figure 232

Nathaniel Spear, Jr., Figures 30 and 31, 32, 40, 41, 43, 55 and 56, 57 and 58, 59, 60, 61, 89, 91 and 92, 151, 219, 220, 268, 298–299

Taylor & Dull, Inc., Figures 6, 39, 46, 47, 54, 62–70, 71–73, 76–87, 88, 149, 152 and 153, 190 and 191, 228–230, 234 and 235, 238, 239, 240, 262, 275 and 276

Ann Britt Tilia, Figures 34, 35, 37, 38

Maps by Francis & Shaw, Inc.

Staff of Chanticleer Press:

President: Paul Steiner
Editor-in-Chief: Milton Rugoff
Managing Editor: Gudrun Buettner
Project Editor: Mary Suffudy
Art Associates: Deryl Dunn, Dolores R. Santoliquido
Production: Ray F. Patient